The Enduring
CHURCH

Christians
in CHINA and Hong Kong

Gail V. Coulson

with Christopher Herlinger and Camille S. Anders

FRIENDSHIP PRESS • NEW YORK

Scripture quotations are from the New Revised Standard Version of the Bible, copyright 1989 by the Division of Christian Education of the National Council of the Churches of Christ in the USA. Used by permission. All rights reserved.

Papercuts are by Chinese Christian artists from Nanjing Theological Seminary. Photographs are from Gail V. Coulson unless otherwise noted.

Copyright © 1996 by Friendship Press

Editorial Offices:
475 Riverside Drive, New York, NY 10115

Distribution Offices:
P.O. Box 37844, Cincinnati, OH 45222-0844

Library of Congress Cataloging-in-Publication Data

Coulson, Gail V.
    The enduring church : Christians in China and Hong Kong / Gail V.
Coulson, with Christopher Herlinger and Camille S. Anders.
        p.   cm.
    Includes bibliographical refrences.
    ISBN 0-377-00306-9
    1. Christianity—China.   2. Communism and Christianity—China.
3. Christianity—Hong Kong.   4. Hong Kong—Social conditions.
I. Herlinger, Christopher.   II. Anders, Camille S.   III. Title.
BR1285.C68   1996
275.1'0825—dc20   95–51999
                                                                CIP

Contents

ACKNOWLEDGMENT

The editors wish particularly to thank Jean Woo, former China Program coordinator of the National Council of the Churches of Christ in the USA, and Diane Allen and the Rev. Ewing W. Carroll, Jr., of the Asia Pacific Region of the World Division of the General Board of Global Ministries, the United Methodist Church, for their invaluable contributions to this book.

Introduction

It used to be said that when a Chinese converted to Christianity, it meant "one more Christian, one less Chinese." While that adage was a distorted generalization about deep and meaningful religious experiences, it contained that grain of truth based on historical realities. For centuries, Christianity was a Western implant, brought to the shores of the Middle Kingdom by well-meaning but often ill-prepared Christian missionaries, who, by turns, were committed, socially aware, arrogant, and naive, and who tried to instill not only the practices and traditions of Western faith but Western cultural, economic, and political traditions as well.

That the Chinese Christian church has endured and even prospered during the almost five decades since the Communist victory of 1949 and the departure of Western missionaries says something of the durability of religious faith and witness to God's steadfastness and the sheer vitality of Chinese Christianity. The Chinese church, long a recipient of the West's paternalistic missionary movement and the victim of much internal suppression during the Cultural Revolution, has come into its own. Perhaps nowhere is this more apparent than in China's rural areas, where most Chinese continue to live. Here, the church is growing most rapidly, its vitality displayed in numbers that the old Western missionaries would have envied. In 1949 there were fewer than 1 million Protestant Chinese Christians. Today, there are more than 12 million.

How this transformation came about is a central part of *The Enduring Church* (chapters 1 and 2), and in its telling, the authors hope to help reverse the traditional roles of mission that have so bedeviled the relationship between the churches of China and those of the West (chapter 4). Christians in China have a story to tell, and there is much Western Christians can learn, in partnership, from them: the meaning of faith amid political change and turmoil; the importance of lay leadership; the need for forgiveness for those who have opposed the mission of the church; the challenge women pose for a church still dominated by men; the need for bridging a serious generation gap within the church; the appreciation of

1

the beauty of simplicity in worship and religious practice. Perhaps their most important gift, however, may be their sense of unity. At a time when the Western church is experiencing new divisions over social, ethical, and moral issues, Chinese Christians—in their commitment to a theologically and culturally diverse but basically uniting church—can light a path for others, showing how those oft-used words "unity in diversity" are not another catch phrase of the moment but can have real meaning.

Still, the diversity of the Chinese experience cannot be underscored enough. Too often portrayed or seen in the West as a monolithic nation and culture, China itself defies easy generalizations, particularly during a time of transition and rapid change. What may be true in Shanghai may not be true in a rural village in Hunan, and what may be true in mainland China will almost certainly not be true in Hong Kong.

Hong Kong's special experience remains another key part of this volume (chapter 3). As a unique stream of Chinese culture and history, now facing the challenge of losing its colonial status in 1997 and becoming reintegrated with the People's Republic of China, Hong Kong is already capturing more of the world's attention. What precisely will happen before, during, and after 1997 is anyone's guess. But Christians both in Hong Kong and on the mainland know that their fates are now increasingly connected. Theirs is a partnership that has distinct parts and histories, but whose combined experiences make up the larger history of Christianity in China—a legacy of faith that is now part of the identity of what it means to be Chinese in Hong Kong and in the People's Republic of China.

This may be a story of triumph, but it is also a story of continued problems from both within and without the church. Even with the astonishing pace of church growth in recent years, Christianity will remain a minority religion in a country of more than 1 billion. If the question facing Chinese Christians is no longer "Whither the church?" it may be, "What faithful role can we play in a society that is changing so rapidly?" It is not a question that yields easy answers. Questions of faith rarely do. But Christians in China and Hong Kong are asking such questions deeply and with hope, mindful that their unique experiences are the most recent history of a growing church, a faithful church, and an enduring church.

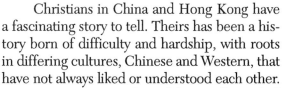

Chapter 1

China and the Church to 1979

Christians in China and Hong Kong have a fascinating story to tell. Theirs has been a history born of difficulty and hardship, with roots in differing cultures, Chinese and Western, that have not always liked or understood each other.

For centuries, China felt a well-justified sense of superiority to the rest of the world. In tracing its roots to the first Chinese civilization in the Yellow River region (about 2700 B.C.), and extending through a 4,000-year history, imperial China, or the Middle Kingdom, could lay claim to a proud tradition: a strong central government; rich currents of painting and calligraphy, literature, music, religion, philosophy, and mathematics; and a sophisticated agricultural society based on family ties and imperial loyalty.

But internal tensions also marked China's history: waves of invasions from the north and west; a stratified society; and gross social injustices and inequalities, particularly against the poor and women of all classes. By the time an expanding and emboldened West began imposing its colonial system throughout the world in the 16th century, China's inner contradictions were becoming more apparent. When Hong Kong became a colonial outpost in the 19th century, China was in a much weakened state—a shadow of its former self.

Imperial China and the West

Disrupting social systems across the globe, Western European colonization gained momentum during the Industrial Revolution. It looked for new markets for exporting machine-produced goods and importing raw materials for Europe's growing cities and factories. Great Britain proved most conspicuous in its empire building. Even the loss of the 13 colonies in North America in the late 1700s couldn't alter the fact that Britain—as a dominant maritime power—amassed an empire that stretched from Canada and the Caribbean in the Western Hemisphere all the way to South Africa, India, and Australia in the east. Steamships, supported by Britain's abundant coal industry and strategic coaling stations around the world, reinforced British naval supremacy in the 19th century.

The British shared global power with other European countries. The Dutch held colonies throughout Asia and occupied Taiwan for a time, bringing with them Protestant clergy, who unsuccessfully attempted conversions. The French, meanwhile, colonized much of Indochina and introduced Catholicism there. But it was the British who became most associated with the burgeoning reality and ideology of colonial expansion.

Political Incursions and the Opium Wars

This growing empire needed to maintain contact with China. In 1793 George McCartney was sent to Beijing to negotiate trading rights for Britain. The Chinese government granted only a minimum of trade, insisting that the Middle Kingdom was self-sufficient. China also tended to disapprove of the accompanying Christian missionary influence, since the propagation of Christianity seemed to threaten or weaken such traditional Confucian values as veneration of ancestors and loyalty to the emperor, the backbone of imperial China.

Despite these Chinese protestations against foreign encroachment, Western powers proved durable and commanding. In the 1830s British merchants desired to expand trade more broadly along the Chinese coast. They set their sights on a fishing village called Hong Kong, located on a rocky offshore island in the South China Sea. The stage was set for a confrontation that altered China's relationship with the rest of the world.

The two Opium Wars of the mid-19th century served as military campaigns to broaden Britain's trade and territory. China believed Britain needed China more than China needed Britain. China wanted little from Britain in exchange for Chinese tea and silk. Wool was hardly in demand in the hot, humid south, and China grew its own cotton. As a result, Britain counteracted its unfavorable trade balance with China by shipping in opium from India. The revenue from selling opium bought tea and silk, which British merchants sent back to London and sold at a profit throughout Europe.

China grew angry. It had banned the production and trading of opium because of the gross social disruption caused by opium addiction, which not only could result in mental deterioration and death to the opium smoker but also disrupted the family who depended on him. China also resented seeing its own trade surplus diminish while foreign traders became wealthy. British traders meanwhile ignored the ban and smuggled the drug into China.

THE DRUG SCENE

If China overcame its drug problem in the past, it is back with a vengeance today. As Deng Xiaoping once said of the Open Door policy, "When you open a door, you'll get more than fresh air, some flies will come in, too!" In June 1995 China commemorated the 156th anniversary of the 1839 bonfire of drugs ordered by the Qing dynasty official Lin Zexu. In the 1995 ceremony, more than 167 kilograms of heroin, morphine, and opium were burned outside Guangdong's Opium War Museum in Humen. China initiated a war against drug trafficking throughout the country, including major crackdowns and prosecutions in Guangdong and Shanghai, as well as condemnations of suspected smugglers and executions of those convicted in Guanxi, Yunnan, and Hubei.

In 1839 the Chinese government demanded that foreign traders, law-breaking Chinese officials, educated gentry, and merchants all surrender their opium. It confiscated and publicly burned 20,000 chests brought into Guangzhou (Canton) by the British. The British responded by dispatching 16 warships and 4,000 troops to demand an apology for the treatment of British traders in Guangzhou. During the First Opium War (1839-42) the British fleet clashed with Chinese war junks in the waters of Hong Kong. As the result of British victory, Britain not only received compensation for the opium; it also forced the Chinese to open additional ports for foreign trade.

Thus began a century of humiliation and hostility against foreign "barbarians"—a resentment exacerbated when the British stepped up their attacks in Guangzhou, seized land in Tianjin, and, in the Treaty of Chuanbi (1841), gained the island of Hong Kong in perpetuity. The British flag had already been planted, and the British takeover of the island had

Ancient pines, crags, and mist reflecting Daoist respect for nature

already begun when, ironically, Lord Palmerston, the British foreign secretary, derided Hong Kong as "nothing more than a barren rock with hardly a house on it" and annulled the treaty. (Palmerston also wasn't happy that the treaty ignored the demand for opening more ports.) Palmerston was only partially right: Though considered uninviting and ill-suited for settlement by the many Chinese, Hong Kong then had some 3,500 inhabitants.

However, Hong Kong's natural anchorage made it a natural center along the Far East trade route. With its superb harbor and its access to the Pearl River, Hong Kong could no longer be dismissed as a mountainous rock that lacked fertile soil and drinking water—it provided easy access to an increasingly weakened China. A second show of British naval force under Henry Pottinger, later knighted and appointed the first governor of Hong Kong, forced the Chinese emperor to sign a treaty that met Palmerston's demands. With the taking of Nanjing in 1842 and the signing of the Treaty of Nanking, China suffered a humiliating defeat—five major ports (Guangzhou, Xiamen [Amoy], Fuzhou, Ningbo, and Shanghai) were open to trade with foreigners. Foreign merchants and government agents entered these ports, along with Christian missionaries, who bought land and opened schools. Though they brought with them a new evangelical zeal, these were not the first Christians in China.

Christianity in China

Imperial China honored a rich variety of religious and philosophical traditions. Daoism, indigenous to China, advocated harmony with nature and the balance of opposite forces called yin and yang. Confucianism, transmitted by the teacher Confucius in the fifth century B.C., was an ethical and political philosophy that stressed relationships characterized by respect for authority. Such respect was expressed in rigid social etiquette in the family, the clan, and the nation. Buddhism, brought by monks from India in the first century A.D., encouraged devotion to Buddha and the saints and set a high value on compassion. Over the centuries, Confucianism accepted the challenge of Daoism and Buddhism and developed its own vital cosmology and metaphysics in the Neo-Confucianism of the Song dynasty. Islam, which arrived from central Asia in the seventh century, proclaimed faith in Allah and obedience to his prophet, Muhammad. Intertwined with these traditions was folk religion, which included devotion to ancestors, spiritual healing, fortune telling, and geomancy (*fengshui*), a technique for situating buildings and tombs in auspicious sites that are in harmony with the environment and out of the path of evil spirits.

Christianity was another of these religious traditions. The first Christian missionaries were the Nestorian monk Alopen and other monks, who arrived from Asia Minor and Persia in 635. The Tang emperor approved the establishment of their churches and monasteries. The Chinese called their faith Da Qin Jing Jiao (the Illustrious Religion of the Great Mediterranean). After the government closed all monasteries, Buddhist and Christian, in 845, Nestorian Christianity gradually disappeared, except for a huge stone tablet carved with the story of Alopen's mission.

Four centuries later, the Franciscan friars arrived. In 1289 Kublai Khan, the Mongol emperor of China, granted permission to the friar John of Montecorvino to do mission work in China. In 1294 the church was formally founded, with John as the first archbishop of Beijing (Peking). The collapse of the Mongol (Yuan) Dynasty in 1368 led to the collapse of the Franciscan missions as well because they were associated with the hated Mongols.

Altar in a Buddhist Temple

Two hundred years later Christians reestablished a presence in China. The arrival of Matteo Ricci and other Jesuit priests in Guangdong Province in 1582 marked an important shift in the relationship between China and the West. The Jesuits introduced Western science, mathematics, and astronomy in 1601 to the Ming court and secured their position as leaders in China. The Middle Kingdom could no longer blithely dismiss outsiders as barbarians who had nothing to offer the Chinese.

The Jesuit experience in China was only one example of the complexities that arise when a religion that is the product of one culture encounters the traditions of another culture. In the resulting interaction, neither side remains unchanged. As the Chinese court gained glimpses of Western knowledge, the Jesuits were attempting to make Christianity more acceptable to the Chinese. They used classical Chinese names of divinities for the single Christian God, they accepted traditional veneration of ancestors as a cultural rather than a religious practice, and they adjusted the liturgy so as not to offend against Chinese customs. Already recognized at court and well-read in the Chinese classics, they felt better equipped as missionaries than Dominicans and Franciscans, who arrived later on the scene and tended to think that the Christian message lost something by accommodating to Chinese culture. These problems surfaced in the Rites Controversy between 1645 and 1724. The Vatican settled it by prohibiting veneration of ancestors for Chinese Catholics and ordering the Jesuits to conform. In retaliation the Qing emperor expelled all Christian missionaries. As a result, Catholic influence waned.

The growing political and economic power of predominantly Protestant nations such as Britain, the Netherlands, and, eventually, the United States made it impossible for China to keep missionaries at bay for very long. Protestant missionary zeal went hand in hand with the expansion of economic and political empires. By the early 1800s, Protestant missionaries began arriving in China—the fourth major effort in a thousand years to Christianize China. Within a century their influence would far exceed their numbers.

In a telling detail, the first Protestant missionary, the Scottish Presbyterian Robert Morrison, arrived in China in 1807 but not on a British ship: the East India Company did not welcome missionaries. (Later Morrison acted as translator for the company, which provided him housing in Guangzhou and the Portuguese colony of Macao, established in 1557.) Instead, Morrison arrived on an American ship and lived with Americans who supported Protestant mission work in China. American missionaries proved themselves the most prominent in mission work during the next century. Elijah and Eliza Bridgman, the first American missionaries in China, arrived in Guangzhou in 1830; their task, that of "Christianizing China," was never easy. Though history records the baptism of the first Chinese convert, Cai Gao, in 1814, 25 years after the first Protestant missionary arrived, there were only 10 baptized Christians.

Moreover, as the late China historian John K. Fairbank noted, the Christian missionaries struggled against tremendous obstacles, including the Chinese language. The missionaries needed terminology to convey their message. China already had a distinctive theological vocabulary to designate God, the soul, sin, repentance, and salvation. But if the missionaries used established terms, usually derived from Buddhism, they could not make Christianity distinctive. They struggled even to come up with a term for God. After much discussion, the Catholics chose the term *Tianzhu* (Lord of Heaven), while Protestants used *Shangdi* (Supreme God or Heavenly King), *Shen* (God), or *Zhu* (Lord).

The Unequal Treaties and the Growth of Foreign Missions

In addition to securing Hong Kong for Britain and opening up China's major ports for foreign trading, China's defeat in the Opium War also meant that China had to pay an indemnity of $21 million in silver and agree to reduced import tariffs. Therefore, foreign goods gained an advantage in local markets. Meanwhile, illegal opium sales continued unimpeded, and additional countries—the United States and France—joined in making new demands of China. In 1844 the United States forced the Qing (Manchu) government to agree that any concession given to one nation automatically be applied to all. Then the international powers demanded—and received—extraterritorial rights and privileges, a violation of the traditional code of the Qing dynasty, which insisted that foreigners abide by the same laws as the Chinese. As a result, foreigners became subject to the laws of their respective nations. These and the other Unequal Treaties ushered in what the Chinese have called the "century of humiliation" and resulted in the growth of foreign enclaves in China's coastal cities, particularly Shanghai, where foreigners could live seemingly unaware that they were in China. Today, Shanghai's varied Western-style architecture stands as historical testimony to that time, as do the memories of affronts like the park signs that once read "No Dogs or Chinese Allowed."

Churches, as well as Western governments and businesses, benefited from this blatantly unequal relationship. Churches in the United States, particularly, felt anxious to spread the gospel beyond the expanding borders of their own country. As domestic missions pushed toward the Pacific, a sense of "missionary obligation for lands beyond the seas" began to capture the imagination of increasing numbers of U.S. Christians, particularly Protestants. The Methodist Stephen Olin of Wesleyan University, for example, said that "Multitudes of members of the church burn with a desire to have some part in overwhelming idol temples of India and China." The church denominations needed to assist those who wished "to give expression to their irrepressible convictions of duty toward the perishing heathen."

It was time, Olin said, for mission boards to end their partiality towards home missions and to develop foreign mission programs. Others shared Olin's convictions. Fueled by an intense religious fervor throughout the United States at mid-century, college organizations and young people's organizations became increasingly committed to the idea of foreign missions, particularly in China. (This despite the rather daunting fact that, in the 1840s, it typically took four months to journey the 12,000 miles by sea to China.)

Within a short time, mission boards acted on these convictions, and many of them, not surprisingly, established Hong Kong as their base for teaching, evangelism, and church planting in China. The missionaries studied Chinese language and culture in Hong Kong before proceeding into China. The American Baptist Mission, the Southern Baptist Convention, and the London Missionary Society established early bases in Hong Kong. The Roman Catholic Church also established a mission prefecture, and in 1847 the foundations were laid for Hong Kong's Anglican cathedral.

The Taiping Rebellion, Foreign Domination, and Church Growth

The aggression shown by the foreign powers and the betrayal of China by the officials of the Qing court angered many Chinese. The philosopher Fang Tungshu said in 1842 that "The strength of the British lay not in their armaments but in the help they got from Chinese traitors." Such anger fueled the Taiping Rebellion (1850-64), the largest, bloodiest peasant uprising against local gentry and foreign aggression during the Qing dynasty. The rebellion ushered in the rapid rise of nationalism and a half century of instability and turmoil.

Many in the West recognized and even sympathized with the aims of the rebellion, which included political and social reform. However, the British realized that a reformed, strengthened, and centralized China would be more resistant to Western penetration and the expansion of markets for Western goods. Moreover, it was more in Britain's self-interest that it gain privileges for residence, trade, and missionary work. As a result, Britain helped defend Shanghai against the Taiping rebels by supporting the gentry-led local militia. Such a partnership dragged China further into the misery caused by foreign imperialists and its own corrupt upper class.

Intense foreign rivalry for Chinese territory added even more turmoil, though it prevented the outright conquest of China by any one country. China's sovereignty was bombarded from all sides. From the south and west via India and Burma came Britain. From the south via Indochina came France. From the east, in part via the Philippines, came Japan and the United States. Xiamen was made an Anglo-French concession in

Camille S. Anders

Temple of Heaven, Beijing, where the emperor made annual sacrifice

1859. A year later, while Anglo-French soldiers entered Beijing, Russia wrested away Amur Province in the north and also received special privileges in Manchuria. Guangzhou was occupied by Anglo-French forces from 1857 to 1861.

In all this struggle, the British continued to have something of an edge. A dispute over the right of China to inspect a British ship resulted in the temporary lease of land for British soldiers in Kowloon, the peninsula across the harbor from Hong Kong Island. Then came the Second Opium War (1856-60), which pitted China against Britain and France and resulted in British troops entering Beijing and burning the emperor's Summer Palace. This violence forced the Convention of Peking (1860), which converted the lease on Kowloon to an agreement that Kowloon was to be "ceded in perpetuity." With Kowloon and nearby Stonecutter's Island now in its possession, Britain could better control Hong Kong's harbor.

In addition to ceding more and more power to foreign governments, the treaties of this era also gave foreign missionaries the right to live and work in the interior of China (protected, of course, by the laws of their governments) and also granted Catholics additional facilities to carry out

11

their activities in the country. Yet by 1864 there were still fewer than 100 Protestant missionaries in China. Their role and influence on Chinese society, particularly in the deepening social ferment, are still debated among historians. It is true that oppressed Chinese felt some support from missionaries in their struggles against the official and gentry classes, and that in some instances, Christians sowed dissent and caused friction in what was a disintegrating society. It is equally true that other Chinese developed an angry patriotic and nationalistic reaction to missionary attempts to "Westernize" them.

Protestant churches grew slowly but steadily, as Fairbank notes. The number of converts and practicing Christians rose to more than 100,000 by 1900. That was a "mere drop in the Chinese bucket," but the Protestants were great institution builders. In his 1992 study, *China: A New History,* Fairbank describes a group of gifted and idealistic young men who accepted the Western religion, partly because the trinity of industry, Christianity, and democracy seemed to be the secret of Western power and the best way to save China. One of the Western-educated Chinese was Sun Yatsen.

The First Sino-Japanese War and the Boxer Rebellion

As the 19th century drew to a close, rapid changes in technology and industry caused a new kind of imperialism and militarism to emerge. China felt this change most acutely in its relations with an emboldened Japan, which had embarked on an ambitious modernization program. During the First Sino-Japanese War (1894-95), Japan invaded Shandong Province and Manchuria and controlled approaches from the sea to Beijing. In a crushing and humiliating defeat for China, Japan secured the cession of Taiwan, the adjoining Pescadores Islands, and a peninsula in Manchuria. In addition, China was forced to grant trading privileges to Japan, recognize the independence of Korea, China's most important client state, and pay a large indemnity to Japan.

This defeat triggered the beginning of revolutionary activity against the Manchu rulers and simultaneous efforts by the Western powers to receive concessions from the ever weakening Qing dynasty. The West's continued aggression—such as Germany's advance in 1898 into Shandong—coupled with anger over Christian missionary activities provoked the Boxer Rebellion. A mass popular uprising, the Boxer Rebellion was so named after anti-imperial militia forces that believed that the boxing they practiced kept them out of harm's way. Those participating in the uprising were peasants who had suffered from floods and drought in the north, and boatmen who had lost jobs to the Western-built railways.

Christian missionaries, both Protestant and Catholic, became targets of hatred, as did Christian converts, who were condemned for abandoning traditional Chinese customs and adopting a foreign religion. In the ensuing violence, thousands of converts and missionaries were killed. Churches, cathedrals, mines, and railways that had been built by foreigners were sacked and destroyed. Although the Manchu court appeared neutral, it secretly supported the Boxers, and the Empress Dowager Cixi (Tz'u Hsi) ordered that foreigners be killed.

The Qing government made one last attempt at reforming the state and the social system. The "Hundred Days of Reform" of 1898 called for Western-style industrialization that would not discard China's cultural heritage. However, the government's 40 edicts of transformation proved to be too great a change, and the reforms floundered because the governing classes clung tenaciously to their power. The empress dowager, for example, had young reformers executed. By 1900, however, occupation of Beijing by an international force of eight nations forced the Qing court to flee and left the Chinese ruling class in a deep state of crisis.

These events unfolded as Germany, Russia, Britain, and France all seized additional harbors, and Britain also asked for cession of 200 square miles near Hong Kong. China flatly refused but did agree to a 99-year lease. So it was that the New Territories, north of Kowloon, as well as 235 outlying islands, came into British control until 30 June 1997. The furious villagers of the New Territories challenged this agreement; they held meetings in ancestral halls and called for armed resistance. Though Chinese troops were brought in from Guangzhou to handle the skirmishes before the raising of the Union Jack over the New Territories, shouts and gunfire from angry villagers could still be heard in the distance.

The protesting Chinese felt angry about more than the cession of the New Territories. By 1899, China had been divided into dozens of spheres of influence. Foreigners, though frightened by the Boxer Rebellion, remained in as strong a position as ever.

In fact, with the turn of the century and the end to the Boxer Rebellion, a 30-year heyday of missionary work began in which social reforms played a central part. The Maryknoll Society, which sent missionaries to Guangdong Province in 1918, was a notable new Catholic effort. The missionaries encouraged efforts to stop the use of opium, and they helped spread the use of Western medicine, establishing hospitals and clinics. Chinese girls, customarily denied formal education, were brought into primary and middle schools. Missionaries supported efforts to stop the practice of foot binding, which had caused untold pain for generations of upper-class girls and women. It is not as clear how vocal missionaries were, or could have been, in openly opposing female infanticide, which was often practiced in poor families. Such intervention could have cost missionaries their lives, as it was a deep-rooted custom.

In 1907 Protestant missionaries held their Centennial in Shanghai without any Chinese present. A year later the American missionary Arthur H. Smith said, "The Christian church, to get a footing, must get recognized, respected, approved, accepted." The Chinese church, with its roots in a century of turmoil and foreign domination, faced a long struggle ahead for its independence.

"PATHETICALLY FEW BELIEVERS"

Despite the valiant efforts of missionaries, the progress of Christianity in its first years in China proved painfully slow. According to the late Rev. Cai Wenhao (Peter Tsai), president of the Zhejiang Christian Council and principal of Zhejiang Seminary,

For over 140 years before liberation, the first 70 years saw pathetically few believers. The first Christians [were] converted after 7 years. For the first 25 years they won only 10 people. After 70 years of work there were only 13,000 Christians. In the following 70 years, thousands of missionaries came from many countries with huge amounts of money and material resources, but there were only 700,000 Christians by the time of liberation in 1949. The slow growth was mainly due to the fact that as a "foreign religion," the church depended on the power of Western nations. Thus it did not have the favor of the people. On the contrary, the people repeatedly started antiforeign-religion movements to oppose it.

The Republic of China

China's history from 1911 to 1949 encompassed massive change, turmoil, and uprootedness for millions. The hopes for change that had been awakened in the 19th century burst forth in the first 50 years of the 20th, as China experienced further wars, more foreign invasions, the establishment and fall of a republic, revolutionary struggle, and, finally, the establishment of a Communist-led government. Through it all, the churches were caught up in the maelstrom of events.

The Founding of the Republic

The Qing dynasty was finally overthrown on 10 October 1911, and four months later the last Qing emperor, Puyi, abdicated. With the collapse of the old dynasty came new political powers and personalities. The most prominent was Dr. Sun Yatsen, who was elected provisional president of the Republic of China, taking office in 1912. This leader of the first phase of China's revolutionary struggle was a man whose

Memorial to Sun Yatsen, Nanjing

mantle would eventually be claimed by both the Nationalist (Kuomintang) and Communist parties. The son of farmers, Sun was educated at a mission school in Hawaii and a medical school in Hong Kong and was converted to Christianity. He soon turned from medicine to revolution, trying again and again to topple the corrupt Qing dynasty. His dream of a new nationalism had been influenced by Western ideals. Yet he remained a thoroughly Chinese figure, and during his years in exile abroad, he drew support from Chinese throughout the world.

Sun's dreams for a new modern China based on the "three people's principles" of nationalism, democracy, and people's livelihood, were not immediately fulfilled. China remained prey to foreign incursion, and the imperial system was replaced by the strife of rival warlords. "We have neither cohesion nor resistance, we have become scattered grains of sand," Sun said, surveying the Chinese political landscape. He died unexpectedly in 1925, venerated as the father of his country.

The aftershocks of World War I (1914-18) reverberated in China, when, at the Versailles Peace Conference, Japan was given control of Shandong and Manchuria. This decision, coupled with the increasing economic power of the United States in China and throughout the Pacific, sparked resentment among China's intellectuals, students, and workers. Students at Beijing University, aligned with workers, called for an end to China's mistreatment by foreign powers. In bringing new hopes of national liberation to China, the May Fourth Movement of 1919 radically changed the course of Chinese history. Inspired by the successful 1917 Russian Revolution, the movement's participants promoted the idea of a

15

modern, democratic China. They called for an end to Confucianism, the old ethical code, and the old political system, which had resulted in a debilitated China at the mercy of foreign powers.

Though the intellectuals of the movement knew little about Communist ideology, the May Fourth Movement laid the groundwork for the founding of the Chinese Communist Party (CCP), which had its first national congress in 1921. The party stressed the Marxist-Leninist theory of social revolution to be led by an alliance of workers and peasants. This alliance of urban and rural workers proved crucial as the industrial modernization of the 1920s began to change the face of China and urban workers began to protest their mistreatment.

In 1923, for example, the first large-scale industrial strike occurred in Wuhan. In 1925 a Japanese worker killed a Chinese worker at a cotton mill and evaded prosecution. In what became known as the May 30th incident, a Communist-influenced coalition of workers and students protested the killing. In the resulting crackdown, British police in Shanghai killed 13 Chinese and wounded many more; strikes and boycotts spread throughout the country. After seven months of unrest those responsible were dismissed by the British, and an indemnity was paid to the families of the dead and wounded.

In protesting the arrogance of such imperial actions, it wasn't surprising that the Kuomintang (KMT) and the Communists were able to collaborate for a time, though their alliance proved fleeting. Both opposed foreign imperialism and the power of the upper class, both made alliances with the Soviet Union, and both assisted peasants and workers. Mao Zedong and other Communists studied alongside Nationalists at the Huangpu Military Academy near Guangzhou, which had been established by Chiang Kai-Shek, the KMT leader who succeeded Sun. Despite these

Workers building a railway as China hastens to industrialize, by Huang Yanghui (1943)

and other similarities—both Chiang and Mao agreed that China needed a strong central government—there were critical, and very pronounced, differences between the two leaders. Chiang favored unifying China by military means and building strength in cities. Mao, meanwhile, pinned his hopes on organizing China's disaffected peasants. Given these differences, it is not surprising that the Communist Party and the Nationalists competed for the direction of national policy, and that by the mid-1920s, both groups were trying to undercut each other. This rivalry eventually turned into a chasm that deepened into the Chinese civil war.

Civil War and the Second Sino-Japanese War

In 1927 a successful Communist uprising in Shanghai, then dominated by warlords and foreign interests, alarmed the Chinese ruling class. They aligned themselves with Chiang and his conservative military supporters, who also were backed by powerful warlords. This alliance violently suppressed the Communists in Shanghai and, with Chiang as the head of the government based in Nanjing, was recognized and aided by the United States and Britain. That was not surprising since the KMT had claimed Sun's legacy and had taken the Nationalist flag as its own. It was also not surprising given that Chiang's wife professed Christianity and had been educated at Wellesley College. Americans would identify with the Chiangs as devout, Western-oriented leaders, and, for the next 20 years, that view seriously clouded American perceptions of what was actually happening in China.

As the 1930s dawned, a series of civil wars and bloodlettings rocked China, killing at least half a million people. The Nationalist government continued to repress the Communists, and little was done to eradicate the disease, illiteracy, and underemployment that plagued rural China. If that was not enough, Japan, which had had military and business interests in Manchuria since 1905, seized power there in 1931 and began to conquer other parts of the northeast. This action, marking the start of the Second Sino-Japanese War, which continued through World War II, hastened the collapse of the Nationalists and led to the eventual victory of the Communists. Thus, it precipitated the birth of the modern Chinese nation. The years 1911-37 had failed to create a national civil society. A truly unified government had not been established; social, political, and economic injustices continued unchecked; and Japan's aggression put an end to whatever hopes still existed for "gradual" reform.

As the civil war for the control of China, intensified by Japanese hostilities, raged on, the KMT relied more and more on the upper classes; it was clear that the KMT was concerned with only one of Sun's "three principles" of modernization: that of nationalism. The other two, democracy and people's livelihood, were being summarily ignored. As a result, peasants became attracted to the Communist beliefs of a revolutionary force fighting and sacrificing on behalf of the poor. Perhaps no other event symbolized that commitment more than the Long March (1934-35), in which the Communists, fleeing the attacking Nationalists, completed a difficult 6,000-mile retreat from the Hunan-Jiangxi border region to the mountains of Yanan, a poverty-stricken backwater in Shaanxi Province. Crossing 18 mountain ranges and 24 rivers, and facing numerous land and air attacks, the Communists lost more than half their number. During this trek Mao rose to undisputed leadership of the CCP. The Long March continues to be celebrated in stories, films, and plays as the most heroic phase of the Chinese Revolution, a time of dedication, self-sacrifice, and spirit during which nationalism combined with social transformation to address the grievances of the rural poor.

Such internal strife was not all that ailed China. Foreign domination continued unabated: in 1936, two-fifths of all China's coastal and river cargo was still carried under the British flag. Britain, moreover, sought the cooperation of the United States against Japan, and the resulting Nine Power Pact of 1937 affirmed, on paper anyway, China's sovereignty, independence, and territorial integrity and gave the nine signing nations the right to do business with China on equal terms. Seen more cynically, the pact implied that the United States, Britain, and Japan could jointly control China.

China began to rally a bit at this time. In a bizarre turn of events in Xi'an in December 1936, Chiang Kai-Shek was kidnapped by one of his own dissident generals who wanted him to fight against Japan instead of against the Communists. Zhou Enlai, one of the Communists' leaders and later China's premier, went to Xi'an to plead Chiang's cause—even though Chiang had been responsible for thousands of Communist deaths in the previous 10 years of bloodshed. Chiang was released to initiate a united front against Japan, but on his return to Nanjing, he arrested the general.

Despite their differences, both Communists and Nationalists joined in patriotic resistance. They faced a seemingly implacable enemy; among the most infamous atrocities Japan committed against the Chinese was the pumping of poisonous fumes into tunnels where local people had taken refuge. When Nanjing fell to the Japanese in 1937, up to 300,000 civilians were massacred, and a puppet nationalist government was installed. In 1938, when Guangzhou fell, a huge flood of 750,000 refugees poured into Hong Kong, most of them having nowhere to live but the streets. This was not the first time, nor would it be the last, that Hong Kong would serve as something of an escape valve for a China in turmoil.

China suffered grievously during the war with Japan, and eventually the Nationalist government fled west from Nanjing to establish a wartime capital in Chongqing (Chungking), enduring not only enormous casualties and the loss of national treasures by air bombardment but also staggering inflation and internal corruption. And with Japan fighting on several fronts against the United States and Britain (in the Philippines, Burma, the Dutch East Indies, and a number of Pacific islands), Hong Kong became a target: Japan invaded the colony in 1941 and occupied it until 1945.

If it can be said that World War II had any positive results for China, or at least its government, it was that China gained respect it had not garnered for at least a century. With the 1943 defeat of Japan in Shanghai, the Americans, British, and French renounced their extraterritorial privileges. And with Japan's final defeat in 1945, China was accorded equal status with the major powers, until then resolutely denied her, and was acclaimed one of the victorious "Big Four."

Renewed Civil War

With their common enemy defeated, the political differences between Communists and Nationalists proved too deep to maintain harmony. The Communists continued to promote social revolution in the countryside, while the Nationalists wished to prevent it. The stage was set for the final phase of the Chinese civil war.

As an ally, the United States urged the Nationalists to work with the Communists while it still continued to furnish the Nationalists with arms and equipment. The Communists denounced the United States for that contradiction, saying it was interfering in Chinese affairs to force Chiang to accept reforms and stop the revolution.

By 1947, it was clear that the Communists were a force to be reckoned with. A year earlier they had formed the People's Liberation Army and by the end of 1949, they had taken Nanjing, Shanghai, and Guangzhou. Their success was largely due to the redistribution of land to peasants in the countryside. As peasants overcame their fears of the local gentry and their traditional respect for property rights, the rural base of the Nationalists was weakened. Peasants seized landlords' properties with unleashed fury and hatred, punishing them and their Nationalist supporters and killing many. The Communists were not able to control extremists and thus alienated many middle-rank peasants. It was a terrifying time, but for those benefiting from the redistribution, there was no turning back.

The Nationalists began preparing to flee, with Chiang transferring most of the government's gold reserves, as well as the air force and navy, to Taiwan. However, the Nationalists were still not prepared to surrender, and the United States, unable to broker a peace between the Nationalists and the Communists, extricated itself from the collapsing Nationalist government. One American general said the United States was "allied to a corpse." The Chinese government was so weakened that it was unable to stem the horrors of rampant inflation in which huge sacks of bank notes were required for even the most trivial purchases.

In 1949 the Nationalists established themselves on Taiwan: a total of 2 million refugees poured into the island. During the last years of the civil war, nearly that many had already flowed into Hong Kong. (Hong Kong's population rose from 600,000 in 1945 to 2.3 million by the mid-1950s.) With Chiang as the head of a government maintained with U.S. aid and assistance, the KMT established a perch from which it vowed to take over the mainland. Thus began a reunification dilemma that has yet to be resolved, and thus began, too, a sour time in American politics, when anti-Communist hysteria was fanned by the question, "Who lost China?"—as if China were anybody's to lose.

The Churches Under the Republic

Given the ever changing relations between the United States and China over the years—with their attendant ups and downs, tensions and misunderstandings—it may be difficult to appreciate fully how much the experience of Christianity in China colored the United States' attitude toward China. Typical of the American attitude was that of Henry Luce, publisher of *Time* magazine. Born in China the son of American missionary parents, he was in large part responsible for the worshipful image of the Chiangs, and he helped perpetuate the view of so many Americans that China was their particular sphere of interest.

The historian Barbara Tuchman noted: "As a result of a century of missionary effort, Americans felt a responsibility for China which they did not feel for other countries. Whether or not the missionaries had made an impact on China, commented a European observer, 'they certainly made an impact on the United States.' " Americans rallied to the Chiangs' defense, Tuchman said, because their leadership of China seemed to provide "such gratifying proof of the validity of the missionary effort."

Yet the Nationalist government's relationship with Christian missionaries was not a simple one. In 1933 the Chiangs had asked American missionaries about undertaking a rural construction campaign in Jiangxi at government expense. The proposal went nowhere, and in 1934 Chiang reinstated Confucianism as the state philosophy.

During the years of the Republic, there were stirrings of a movement for independence from foreign mission boards among the various Chinese

The young Mao Zedong talking to peasants

Protestant churches. Independent churches, such as the True Jesus Church, appeared in more than 600 places. In 1922 the First National Chinese Christian Conference was called as a clearing house for more than 100 foreign mission boards active in China. At its Shanghai meeting it called for the indigenization of Chinese Christianity and elected a Chinese pastor, Cheng Jingyi, general secretary. Crossing denominational lines, the Presbyterian and Congregational churches and the London Mission Society merged to form the Church of Christ in China in 1927. Another milestone was the 1948 election of a Chinese theologian, T. C. Chao (Zhao Zichen), as one of the presidents of the World Council of Churches. Despite these signs of indigenization and unification, it was clear that most of the churches in China were still dependent on missionary support from Western denominations.

The question of independence would be renewed after liberation when the churches would be among those institutions most challenged in what was to be a radically altered political, economic, and social landscape.

The People's Republic

"The Chinese people have stood up!" Party Chairman Mao declared in Tiananmen Square when the People's Republic was founded 1 October 1949. Centuries of foreign domination, interference, and privilege had ended. A new kind of society would be created. In the face of this antiforeign atmosphere, Westerners—including missionaries—fled or were expelled in massive numbers. China became diplomatically isolated from the West as it was refused entry into the United Nations in 1950

Mao Zedong, Communist Party chairman

and sided with Communist North Korea against the United States, South Korea, and other nations in the Korean War of the 1950s.

Socialist Reconstruction

During these years of isolation, China turned inward. The new government embarked on a program of development, national assertion, and anti-imperialism. Perhaps nowhere was this program more needed than in China's most populous city—and the one most associated with foreign domination. The end of the war found Shanghai in chaos: inflation ran rampant and there were no plans for industrial reconstruction. (Still, at long last, signs in the parks that read "No dogs or Chinese" could be removed.)

In these years China worked hard to eradicate economic and psychological legacies of the past. In 1950 it passed the Marriage Law, which gave women the right to divorce and promoted greater equality between the sexes. The state began the systematic acquisition of private property and redistributed it to landless peasants. It also created new systems of food distribution, a national health service, and state schools open to all by examination. The new order emphasized internal regional development, moving factories away from coastal cities into the interior. This policy was taking a cue from the Soviet Union; when Sino-Soviet relations cooled in 1960, it was reversed. To improve agriculture and reshape people's thinking, the state organized them into village and regional associations, dominated by party cadres (core groups of trained leaders) and disciplined by People's Tribunals that

Krystin Granberg

Children in a private nursery school

Jin Wei with children in a program of the Shanghai YMCA

denounced , imprisoned, and executed at least 1 million Chinese as "enemies of the people."

Meanwhile, in factories, workers were encouraged to reveal their superiors' long-standing malpractices of bribery, tax evasion, and illegalities. Managers had to confess their wrongdoings and engage in political reeducation. Some faced harsher measures, such as heavy fines. Indeed, this was a time when the old elite had to choose whether or not to support the new order.

Private enterprise that was not foreign dominated or comprised of corrupt members of the old social structure was allowed to continue if "utilized, restricted, and reformed." Eventually, private enterprises became state-run businesses. While the motto "serve the people" took hold in the popular consciousness, the system did not necessarily lead to productivity. One reason was that the state-run distribution system, known as "eating from one big pot," allowed businesses to stay in operation even if they weren't profitable. As a result, even workers who performed badly or who sat and chatted during working hours collected pay and bonuses.

Swing to the Far Left and the Great Leap Forward

From 1957 to 1966 a new period of bold leftist experimentation took root in the country. In 1957 Mao accused those who criticized collectivization and the new educational policies of being rightists and following the capitalist line. Many were arrested. A year later, the concept of large "people's communes" replaced the smaller cooperatives of peasant land organized in 1955-56, and fully socialist collectives were promoted.

These developments were harbingers of the Great Leap Forward of 1958, when the government tried to form new social units consisting of several thousand households each, in an effort to catch up with industrialized nations before the end of the century. Many households set up backyard furnaces to try to produce steel. The experiment was a horrendous disaster, requiring drastic rehabilitation of the economy and causing enormous economic loss, disorganization, and waste. The situation was made worse by a series of floods and droughts, leading to widespread starvation, and by the termination of Soviet aid. The resulting chaos caused some 20 million deaths.

The Churches in the New China

Christianity in the New China was fundamentally transformed as society was forcibly converted from a free-enterprise, capitalist economy to a state-controlled socialist economy. For approximately the first 15 years the Communist government, although officially atheist, tolerated religious freedom Some Western missionaries returned to China after World War II; some left after liberation in 1949, but some lingered into the early 1950s. Some Chinese Christians stayed aloof from politics. Others, lamenting "one more Christian, one less Chinese," set out to reconcile patriotism with religion, political ideology with faith, by working for the indigenization of the church.

Their efforts were strengthened by the Young Men's Christian Association (YMCA) and the Young Women's Christian Association (YWCA), organizations that had long been sympathetic to the Communist revolution and had Chinese leadership. The Y's offered free classes in literacy, vocational training, sports, and health. Such Y leaders as Y. T. Wu, Liu Liangmo, Tu Yuqing, and Cora Deng encouraged church leaders to support the Chinese Protestant Three-Self Patriotic Movement (TSPM), which emphasized self-government, self-support, and self-propagation. The "Chinese Manifesto," written by Y. T. Wu in 1950 and signed by some 400,000 Chinese Christians by 1952, expressed these principles. The move toward independence intensified during the Korean War as the government made it necessary for Western missionaries who had remained in China independently to leave the country. The U.S. government froze China's assets, thus blocking mission funds.

The tendency toward independence was accompanied by a move toward unity in place of denominational divisions. The continued use of large and grandiose Protestant church and school buildings remaining from before 1949 caused a tremendous drain on scarce personnel and financial resources, which the now self-supporting churches could not afford. Some churches closed their building and congregations of different denominations consolidated their worship. In 1952, 12 independent theological seminaries in eastern China united to form Nanjing Union Theological Seminary, and the next year 13 seminaries in the north merged to become Yanjing Union Theological Seminary. Yanjing joined Nanjing in 1961. The school's theology ranged from fundamentalist and conservative to liberal and ecumenical. Jiang Peifen, an evangelical member of the faculty, said of her experience there,

In the past I thought my faith was the most pure. I held the truth in my hands, while others with a different tradition meant nothing to me. I thought too that my prayers were the most ardent, while others were not as sincere. In those days [before 1949] each denomination went its own way, without much to do with one another. Later, after liberation, the opportunities to come in contact with one another increased, not so much in the religious context but in other areas. . . .

Every time I listen to others I learn something that I did not know before. In this manner my faith has been broadened. My knowledge of Christ has been enriched. We receive from God very different gifts. As we come together we not only enrich one another, but also help one another grow. There are still those who want to keep a distance. But with mutual respect the church in China is no longer divided.

ELDER SISTER JIANG PEIFEN

Jiang Peifen (1914-1995) was called Elder Sister by other Christians not because she belonged to a religious order (she didn't) but because they held her in such high esteem. She taught in Zhonghua Seminary in Shanghai before 1949, at a time when it was unusual for a Chinese woman to have an academic position. In 1950 she moved to Nanjing to serve in a local church and in 1956 she joined the staff of the newly formed, nondenominational Nanjing Union Theological Seminary. In 1987 with the assistance of Peng Cui'an, later to become vice principal of the seminary, she organized the first one-year theology program to train lay workers in rural areas. This pilot program became a model followed by many regional and provincial seminaries.

The Korean War and the U.S. embargo on trade to China led to the estrangement of Chinese Christians from North American Christians and the severing of relations with the World Council of Churches. But these losses were balanced by the gains of independence and unity.

Since its earliest days, the Chinese Communist Party (consisting of less than 4 percent of the population) espoused the policy of a United Front of all the peoples of China, including intellectuals, workers, women, ethnic minorities, and religious believers. Together they would work to build the New China. Accordingly, the Constitution of 1954 guaranteed religious freedom to five officially recognized "basic religions"—Daoism, Buddhism, Islam, Catholicism, and Protestantism—so long as they did not try to subvert the government. It also established a Religious Affairs Bureau (RAB) to represent the government in the implementation of religious policy. That same year the First National Christian Conference was held in Beijing. At that time there were about 900,000 Protestants and 3.2 million Catholics out of a population of 500 million.[1]

As foreign funds were cut and ties to mission boards were severed, the Chinese Protestant Three-Self Patriotic Movement was established as an organization in 1954 to replace denominational structures. Catholics faced a more difficult transition because bishops had to be appointed by Rome. Also Pope Pius XII had declared that any Catholics who supported the Communist government would be excommunicated. The government persecuted many Chinese Catholics, believing they were "antirevolutionary." By 1958, many bishops had died or been forced to leave, resulting in a shortage of leaders. To supply that need, Chinese Catholic priests elected and consecrated new Chinese bishops, despite Vatican disapproval. Meanwhile, Protestant churches dismantled denominational structures without eliminating differences in beliefs and practices. In 1960 the Second National Christian Conference was held. In 1962 the Second Conference of the Chinese Catholic Patriotic Association met in Beijing.

The relative security that churches enjoyed during this period of Chinese history was swept away during the Cultural Revolution.

The Cultural Revolution

Launched by Mao Zedong in 1966 to revive his plummeting popularity after the failure of the Great Leap Forward, the Great Proletarian Cultural Revolution was initially a way to combat "revisionism"—revising or defeating the initial goals of the revolution. Few understood the term, but what resulted was a revolutionary zeal that brought turmoil to China for a full decade. It caused great harm to industry, agriculture, education, the arts, religion, and the pursuit of free expression in all areas of life.

Mao planned to purge an older generation of leaders and replace them with a new generation filled with revolutionary zeal. As the chairman put it, "You learn to swim by swimming, you learn to make revolution by making revolution." The most turbulent phase of the Cultural Revolution began in May 1966, when university students began to turn on their teachers. Mao supported them, and in particular a Qinghua University group calling itself the Red Guard. In the name of destroying the "four olds"—outdated ideas, old culture, old customs, and old habits—young people formed further units. They created havoc throughout the country, acting largely in unison and gaining inspiration from the little red book *The Thoughts of Chairman Mao*. National treasures of art and literature carefully handed down for hundreds, or even thousands, of years were destroyed. Temples, churches, mosques, universities, and other institutions were sacked.

Countless Chinese suffered greatly, losing homes and jobs (being sent to work with peasants in the fields for reeducation) or even their lives. Victims of such persecution included party cadres, bureaucrats, technical experts, artists, intellectuals, university professors and school teachers, and people of all religious faiths. Most were accused of being "reactionary and bourgeois." Numerous veteran revolutionaries were wrongly accused of being "capitalist roaders." Chinese who returned from overseas were suspected of being "foreign agents."

The Cultural Revolution began to subside in 1969, but excesses continued. The turmoil finally settled following Mao's death in 1976 and the arrest that same year of the "Gang of Four," including Mao's widow, Jiang Qing. The four were tried and sentenced in 1981, and from city to countryside, countless Chinese citizens celebrated the gang's downfall and the end to the devastation they had wrought. Court statistics showed that more than 729,000 people were framed and persecuted and that nearly 35,000 died as a result of the Cultural Revolution. As one China observer said, "There is simply no way to tabulate the many forms of suffering the gang and its followers inflicted upon China." In retrospect, one former Red Guard member said, "By experiencing disaster, my generation did learn one terribly important thing—the danger that lies in blind obedience." China is still trying to recover from this disastrous experience.

However, some Chinese would consider it unfortunate if all aspects of the Cultural Revolution were discarded in the effort to divest Mao's political heritage of errors and distortions. Among the positive aspects were encouragement of participatory initiatives from below; abolition of the different status traditionally accorded to mental and manual labor; egalitarianism; and an improvement in infrastructure, such as the building of the Beijing subway and the Changjang (Yangtze) River bridge in Nanjing. For years after the Cultural Revolution, Christians did not dwell on or theologize about their suffering because they were too busy reconstructing China. As time has passed, there has been more openness in sharing those experiences of hardship and turmoil. Without excusing the hardship and brutality, Chinese church leaders have said, for example, that their understanding of rural people is appreciatively different, after having been sent to work on farms and in villages.

Quiet Persistence

During the Cultural Revolution and for years afterward, all churches were closed. Many were damaged or destroyed; others were converted to schools, warehouses, or factories. Christian leaders, like other religious and intellectual figures, were persecuted. Believers lived in fear of their lives. Many, however, worshiped secretly in their own homes.

The stories of quiet persistence and hope during this time of troubles are reminiscent of tales from the early church in the West, the church of the catacombs. For example, when one church closed, a brave soul took the communion table home with him so it would not be destroyed. The man's son urged him to use the table for ordinary purposes, but the man kept it set aside and returned it when the church opened more than 10 years later.

Members of another church kept for years special bags in which they placed the money they would have donated to the offering if they had been able to go to church. In 1979, on the first Sunday the churches reopened, these faithful Christians took the bags with them to church—not having

In times of trouble, faithful Christians at home

28

missed one Sunday's giving. In still another example, during every Christmas eve of the Cultural Revolution, a woman and her family stood in silence outside their former church, which had then been converted into a warehouse.

The Rev. Wang Weifan, a professor at Nanjing Seminary, has written of this strange era:

> The Cultural Revolution involved the Chinese church and its pastoral workers in the same disaster that the whole Chinese people were experiencing. But following this nearly unbearable suffering, we felt that what we had gained was greater than that which we lost. There was a return to our own people, for we found ourselves•in the same boat throughout the tempest of those 10 years.
>
> Secondly after the heat of the fiery furnace of the 10 years, many of our own imperfections were burned away. Of course, we were not refined to gold, and other imperfections still remain. These experiences in which we "had to become like his brothers and sisters in every respect," enabled the Chinese church to enter into the role of a "merciful and faithful high priest," for our own nation and people (Heb. 2:17).
>
> "The word was here made flesh." "Here" in China we are a people with thousands of years of cultural tradition, a people who have also experienced all the difficulties and vicissitudes of life. And the body of Christ made flesh is the tiny church of China, which has identified with its people in suffering and has built itself up.

The Chinese Constitution of 1975 continued to guarantee freedom to the five basic religions while giving the right to propagate atheism.

Relations with Hong Kong and Taiwan

The new People's Republic did not at first seek to restore its sovereign rights over Hong Kong, which was due to return to Chinese control in 1997. In 1982 China made it clear that it intended to recover Hong Kong "when conditions were ripe." Britain, which had lost much of its former authority after World War II, allowed Hong Kong a large degree of economic autonomy. Hong Kong used this leeway to launch an extensive industrialization program to make up for the U.S. trade embargo imposed on China because of the Korean War. The influx of businesspeople, intellectuals, pastors, lay leaders, and missionaries from China created a large pool of experienced leaders, talents, and resources. Industry thrived— soon the label "Made in Hong Kong" was seen on clothes and other goods all over the world.

The churches also flourished. Local congregations multiplied and did relief and welfare work for less affluent refugees. A number of theological institutions moved from China to Hong Kong to continue training pas-

Precious farmland and encroaching housing

tors and lay workers. The Hong Kong Christian Council was formed in
1954. A vigorous evangelical movement began on college campuses and
became a strong Christian witness among the intelligentsia.

China's relations with Taiwan were strained, since China claimed it
and Taiwan, dominated by Nationalist Chinese from the mainland,
claimed the mainland. The situation eased when China replaced Taiwan in
the United Nations in 1971 and U.S. President Richard Nixon, a long-time
foe of Communism and a supporter of Chiang Kai-Shek, underwent a
political conversion and traveled to China.

With Chiang's death in 1975, the urgency of the Taiwan issue died
down. That and Nixon's visit prepared the way for restoration of full diplomatic relations between the United States and the People's Republic in
1979. The United States severed official ties with Taiwan and U.S. troops
left the island. In 1982 the United States and China signed an accord in
which China agreed to seek reunification by peaceful means and the
United States agreed not to interfere with the internal affairs of China.

Readjustment Toward the Right

The year 1976 led to a time of deep questioning about the course
Chinese Communism should take. Premier Zhou Enlai died in January.
His protégé, vice premier Deng Xiaoping, a veteran of the Long March
and a victim of the Cultural Revolution who was resilient in his ability to

rise in the government hierarchy, stood ready to succeed him. Instead he was removed from office in April at the instigation of Party Chairman Mao, who considered him an "arch unrepentant capitalist roader who wanted to move China into a technologically advanced world without corresponding political and social development according to Marxist and Maoist principles."

When Mao himself died in September, he was widely mourned but also criticized for preferring revolution to the harder task of governing. In April 1977 Deng was reinstated as vice premier, but he quickly became the most powerful man in the country. He told the Eleventh Party Congress that China needed "less empty talk and more hard work." Abandoning many Communist doctrines as incompatible with modernization, he urged a policy of economic reform that included opening China to the outside world. Supporting Deng's views, the Third Plenum of the Eleventh Party Congress, held in December 1978, decided that reform was necessary, thus changing the whole direction of the economy. The hallmark of the new program was the Four Modernizations (of agriculture, industry, science and technology, and defense). Starting first with agriculture, the government introduced the Responsibility System, which moved the economy in the direction of free enterprise. Special Economic Zones were created to attract foreign investment; that policy caused Hong Kong to shift from a manufacturing to a service economy. Coastal areas, rather than the interior, were encouraged to develop quickly.

A key measure of China's shift from a centralized socialist system toward a free-market economy was taken in 1981, when a scant five years after the death of Mao, the administration of avowed anti-Communist U.S. President Ronald Reagan granted China most-favored nation trading status.

During these years of political and economic readjustment, the church in China flourished, as will be described in the next chapter.

---

1. G. Thompson Brown, *Christianity in the People's Republic of China* (Atlanta: John Knox Press, 1983), p. 78.

Chapter 2

Renewal: The Church in China Since 1979

After Communists expelled Western missionaries in the early 1950s, researchers agree, there were fewer than 3.5 million Christians (700,000 Protestants and the rest Catholic) in China. Chinese Christians had a right to ask, "Whither the church?" The question became even more relevant during the 1960s and early 1970s when the Cultural Revolution unleashed its fury against all forms of religion in China. So successful was this persecution that Jiang Qing, Mao Zedong's third wife, pronounced that religion in China was dead.

Or so it seemed. In 1995 the China Christian Council estimated there were between 8.5 million and 12.6 million Protestants in China. There were about 3.5 million Catholics. The council estimates that three new churches open every two days. These figures are conservative, but other estimates of 20 million or 50 million or more are not much more than speculation. As Bishop K. H. Ting (Ding Quangxun) has said, "Christianity has never been [in] as favorable [a position] as it is now." How did this transformation come about and what does it mean for the church?

The Church Renewed

The end of the Cultural Revolution and China's economic liberalization under Deng

Xiaopeng made the 1980s an invigorating period for the churches. In the resulting climate of economic and social uncertainty, many people, especially in the countryside, looked to the churches for spiritual moorings. In these circumstances the churches have experienced unprecedented renewal and restoration.

Anyone who has worshiped with Christians in China cannot fail to be impressed by their vibrancy and faithful witness. Every week millions of believers eager to hear God's word flock to city and country churches alike. The vitality of the church in China is confirmed by sanctuaries so packed that countless worshipers sit on stools in makeshift courtyards listening by loudspeaker. In some urban churches, video equipment transmits the service to overflow rooms for those arriving too late to find seats in the sanctuary. It is not unusual for rural Christians to travel several hours to attend a worship service. They are disappointed when the sermon is less than an hour!

In September 1979, 13 years after it was forced to close, the first Chinese church in Shanghai to be officially reopened was the Mu'en Church. More than 5,000 Christians came forth to worship that fall. Cheng Naishan, a teacher who became an award-winning writer, converted to Christianity that year. As she described it,

One Sunday in 1979, I "chanced" to pass by Mu'en Church. Snatches of a hymn came to my ears. I was attracted by it in spite of myself, and I entered the

Christmas service in Mu'en Church, Shanghai

packed church. All sorts of feelings welled up in my heart, and I did nothing to stop them. Who could have foretold that after the years of turmoil one would be able to hear religious music here? "Holy, holy, holy, Lord God almighty..." The hymn shook me to the core. I believe that this was God calling to me. From then on I went often to church. In addition to the sermon I went to breathe that atmosphere, that peace and tranquillity, that air of love.

By 1983, there were 15,000 to 20,000 worshipers attending 11 reopened Shanghai churches, allaying fears that Christians would be too fearful to worship in public after the trauma of the Cultural Revolution.

THE FIRST CHURCH TO REOPEN IN SHANGHAI

The late Rev. Sun Yanli, senior pastor of Mu'en (formerly Moore Memorial Methodist) Church in Shanghai in 1966, described his experience.

On August 23, 1966, Red Guards stormed into the church. They burned Bibles and hymnals as a revolutionary act and smashed things. I was shut up in a room and told to write self-criticisms until the Religious Affairs Bureau arranged for me to do work in a factory.

Thirteen years later, with the Policy of Religious Freedom reinstated in 1979, I retired from the factory and went back to reopen the church. A middle school occupied the building and we negotiated with them to use the sanctuary on Sunday mornings. We sent out a notice to tell of the first worship service to be held after the Cultural Revolution in Mu'en Church. We were afraid that many would not come.

By God's grace they did, what a thrilling experience! On Sunday 2 September 1979 the sanctuary was full. Those crammed into smaller rooms relied on loudspeakers to hear.

Aiding Sun Yanli was the Rev. Shi Qigui, the senior pastor today. He had graduated from seminary and was ready to serve a church when the Cultural Revolution began. He was sent to a factory. In his long years there he helped an old Buddhist priest, who could hardly manage the heavy work. The priest told him to have faith that he would pastor a congregation one day. When the church reopened, the sanctuary was still being used as a school auditorium during the week. Every Sunday Shi would rise long before dawn in order to cover up the portraits of Mao and other leaders before the congregation, to be sure of a seat, began arriving two hours before the first service at 6:30 A.M.

It took five years of negotiations to get the whole Mu'en church building back, room by room. Later the bell tower, broken down during the Cultural Revolution, was rebuilt. The bells rang out again for the first time on June 26, 1989, the day Sun Yanli was consecrated bishop.

There were at least 500 reopened churches in various Chinese cities. Many more Christians continued to worship in their own homes or to gather in friends' homes, as they had done in the years of persecution. Such house churches were especially common in the country, where there were no church buildings. The Constitution of 1982, on the advice of 14 religious leaders, restated the policy of freedom of belief for China's five recognized religions.

The church came into its own in other ways. The Protestant Three-Self Patriotic Movement (TSPM) reappeared in a large meeting in Shanghai in 1980. It issued an open letter pointing out that not only religious persons but also government officials and intellectuals suffered in the Cultural Revolution. The letter proposed the publication of Bibles and the training of ministers and called on Christians for patriotic support. One of the TSPM's functions was to negotiate with the government for the return of church property and funds.

Also in 1980 the China Christian Council (CCC) was founded to include all Protestant congregations. Its president was Bishop K. H. Ting (Ding Guangxun) from the Anglican tradition. The council sanctioned both church and home worship and was open to friendly relations with churches abroad, although it did not support specific denominations. Nanjing Union Theological Seminary reopened in 1981 under Bishop Ting. It accepted 51 students out of 700 applicants.

The Catholic Bishops' Conference (CBC) was restructured in 1980. The bishops consecrated five new bishops without Vatican approval. The Church Administrative Commission (CAC) was strengthened to serve Catholics.

Recession, Oppression, and the Church

The late 1980s and 1990s witnessed an amazing transformation on the international scene as the Soviet Union underwent *peristroika* and restored diplomatic relations with China (1989), Germany was unified, and the Soviet Union eventually split into its component parts. China was not immune to stirrings for political reforms and liberalization, which had not generally accompanied Deng's economic reforms. In the spring of 1989 thousands of demonstrators, many of them students, flocked to Tiananmen Square in Beijing. Wearied by inflation, high unemployment, and political corruption, the demonstrators called for patriotic reforms.

The government, fearing any opposition as a threat to the security of the state, sent troops and tanks to subdue the demonstrators, resulting in the tragedy of 4 June 1989 in which both demonstrators and soldiers were killed. The crackdown was all the more dramatic given the general hope-

Catholic cathedral at Catholic Seminary, Shanghai

fulness of the era and the new power of global communications. Chinese students faxed their calls for reform throughout the world, and the brutality of the crackdown was televised globally while it happened. Deng's support of the military suppression caused him to lose much prestige abroad and alienated many in China. It was a critical test of his leadership, which many believed he resoundingly failed. In late 1995 Deng was suffering from Parkinson's disease. However history will record his legacy, no one doubts that China is a radically different place because of him.

The years immediately following the Tiananmen Square demonstration were a time of continued political paranoia and suspicion of outside cultural and political influences but with continued acceleration and liberalization of the Chinese economy. Although the administration of President Bill Clinton "de-linked" trade from the issues surrounding China's human-rights record, human rights as perceived in the West continued to bedevil China's international image. Also of concern in the West were sovereignty issues regarding Tibet, a growing military buildup, renewed tensions with Taiwan, and a widening rift with the United States.

Meanwhile, the work of the church continued, though not without new difficulties and challenges. In 1991 the government issued a new directive in which it said that "steps must be taken to counteract hostile religious activities infiltrating from abroad," and new patriotic and socialist education programs were intensified for those practicing religion. Nevertheless, the church was reaching out to the world community. In 1991 the China Christian Council was readmitted to the World Council of Churches at the WCC's assembly in Canberra, Australia. That was a moment to relish. The Chinese church, long the recipient of the West's paternalistic missionary movement and the victim of much internal repression, had come to symbolize the durability and commitment of the Christian faith within a unique Chinese context.

To understand that durability, the following pages will consider more closely the intersection of faith and secular society, particularly the church's relation to the state, its membership and activities, and such issues as the role of women and youth.

Church and State: Peaceful Coexistence

The Constitution of 1982 recognizes the right of China's five religions to exist. How is that right protected by the government and what does it mean in terms of daily Christian life?

Religious Institutions

The church is protected by one governmental and two nongovernmental institutions. The **Religious Affairs Bureau** (RAB), an arm of the State Council, was designed to represent the government in the implementation of religious policy. Specifically it acts as an intermediary between religious bodies and the government. According to Philip Wickeri, Amity overseas coordinator, Christians may appeal to the RAB through the TSPM in cases where they believe their religious freedom has been violated.

Since 1984 the RAB has been conducting training classes for local Party cadres to improve their understanding of religious policy and its implementation. Even so, there have been abuses and needless actions by local cadres to curtail religious freedom as well as interference by government officials in the internal affairs of Christian communities. This situation, together with indiscriminate dissolution of meeting points, has been questioned by church leaders; much work has yet to be done to prevent such occurrences.

The **China Christian Council** (CCC) was formed by the National Christian Conference in 1980 to assist churches in China with spiritual, administrative, and ecclesiastical matters. The CCC works at national, provincial, and local levels to promote unity among Protestants. Its 10 commissions deal with administration, rural work, women, music, international relations, ministry to ethnic minorities, theological education, and Bible printing and other publications. Although it is recognized by the government, it is not the "official church" of China.

The **Three-Self Patriotic Movement** (TSPM) Committee, formed in the 1950s, is also an organization of Protestants. According to its constitution it was established to end control by foreign mission boards and raise a sense of self-respect and patriotic fervor among Christians in the

New China. As a liaison between the RAB and the churches, it is particularly useful in helping pastors negotiate with the government for return
of confiscated church property and relocating previous occupants, a difficult task since unoccupied land and buildings are extremely limited.

Religious Laws

In the recent past religious freedom was sometimes abused, mostly
at the local level by cadres who misunderstood the policy or by misguided
foreigners who thought they had the best way to proclaim the faith. To
reduce the instances of such abuse, the State Council in 1994 issued two
decrees (see Appendix). Decree 144 regulates the conduct of foreigners
in China. Decree 145 regulates the management of religious premises.
Both decrees are essentially welcomed by religious bodies in China
because they provide greater protection by law. Indeed the opinions of
the CCC and TSPM were sought by the government in the drafting stage.
Thus Christians in China are themselves doing the work of the gospel.

THE BIG BELL

*The Dongshan Protestant Church began in 1909 as a Southern Baptist
missionary compound on a barren hill in the eastern suburb of Guangzhou.
Known as Dongshan, or East Hill, the compound included a hospital, primary school, two secondary schools, a seminary, and a Bible school.*

*Shao Mingyao, a church member, told how every Sunday at noon, the
powerful and solemn chime of Dongshan Church in its 75-foot bell tower
called people to worship. It failed to ring in two difficult eras—the Second
Sino-Japanese War, when the Japanese army converted the church into a
military hospital, and the tumultuous Cultural Revolution, when Red
Guards used it to store their confiscated treasures. Other church buildings
were used to detain and torture so-called monsters and demons. For nearly 10 years, Christians in Guangzhou were afraid even to pass by the gates
of Dongshan Church.*

*When the church was returned to its rightful owners, the walls and
fixtures needed repair. Bibles and hymnals had been burned to ashes and
most of the furniture was missing. With the help of the TSPM, local
Christians pooled their wisdom and resources and began extensive renova-
tion. At the reopening the big bell tolled again. Among hundreds of worshipers was 80-year-old Du Shaoqi, a famous medical doctor and devoted
church member. Though in great pain from cancer of the liver, he insisted
on being carried to the reopening service and sang and prayed in a feeble
voice. A few days later, he died peacefully.*

Decree 144 welcomes foreign partners in mission who enter China legally and are open in their being Christian and honest in their intentions. Restrictions are primarily directed toward groups who secretly do evangelistic work in a clandestine manner and who are not welcomed in China as a result of the potential heresies they incite, especially in rural areas.

Decree 145 deals mainly with the management of religious premises and ensures that "the rights to carry out normal religious activities within these premises are protected by law." These premises include churches and "meeting points" (congregations gathering in a house or hall or other nonchurch structure for worship). (Families can also gather to worship in their own homes.)

Within these premises, which are registered with the government much as nonprofit organizations are registered in the United States, religious people have the right to sell religious materials and manage their own monetary affairs. Christians in China agree that there must be additional clarity in the definition of "procedures and criteria" in order to circumvent abuse by ignorant or prejudiced local cadres. The China Christian Council has also suggested that being an adherent of the Three-Self Patriotic Movement not be a criterion for any congregation to register with local authorities. Such a provision would protect groups such as some members of the Little Flock and True Jesus Church that do not accept the TSPM.

Those from outside China generally view "registration" negatively. Bishop Ting provides another view. In a series of interviews he notes that all social organizations in China must register with the government. Because the church is a social as well as spiritual organization it "need not be made an exception." "My feeling is that registration done according to regulations is acceptable to the Christian conscience and that refusal to register does not glorify God and is not helpful to the church," he said. "I believe that the government's objective [is] to ensure social tranquillity, to give protection to normal religious activities, and as far as possible to ensure that undesirable foreign elements have no room for maneuver." Ting also said decrees 144 and 145 were not attempts to crack down on religion.[1]

In 1994 Ting and other leaders told Konrad Raiser, general secretary of the World Council of Churches, that the regulations were the first policies defining religious activities in more than 20 years and that they had to be seen within that historical context. For his part, Raiser said the decrees codified what had been practiced already, and that now authorities could be held accountable for their policies. Chinese church leaders have stressed that this fact was ignored by media accounts of the new laws.

They said Christians welcome the guidelines because there is now a degree of accountability for local officials who have misused their power, often out of ignorance.[2] While some local communities have complained about arbitrary applications of government policy, Raiser said none of the church leaders with whom he met complained about "open infringement of religious liberty."[3]

Edmund Doogue, co-editor of the *Ecumenical News Service,* who traveled with Raiser to China in 1994, notes that the CCC's "dispassionate approach" to the question of government regulations and its willingness to engage in dialogue with the government have resulted in accusations from overseas Chinese and Christians living outside of China that the council is acting as a collaborator with the government.[4] He said such accusations ignore the frequent interventions by Ting and others on the council on behalf of religious believers. Ting has defended those who are not affiliated with the council, calling them "patriotic and law-abiding." Doogue also noted that critics of the council forget that

The Christian community in China must live under a Communist government. While religious freedom has increased since . . . the end of the decade-long Cultural Revolution, the possibility remains of a return to harsher times.

The CCC seems to have carved out for itself a peculiarly Chinese form of Christianity which can exist without compromising its own integrity. Many of the young pastors under the sponsorship of the CCC simply do not question the government regulations. "If the Christian churches do not have good relations with society and with the government, then we won't be able to preach," said Qi Tieying in Beijing, adding that he saw no problem in the present relationship between the CCC and the Beijing authorities.[5]

In a 21 February 1994 statement, the China Christian Council said the decrees represented "no departure from the practices which have existed for years." Of the decree on foreign nationals, a spokesperson said:

We think people are surely reading too much into the document if they surmise it is meant to separate Chinese Christians from their sisters and brothers abroad, or to prevent foreign church people from being invited to preach in Chinese churches or lecture in Chinese theological schools. We do not see any change in the status and work of Amity teachers or church visitors from overseas whom we receive.

The CCC spokesperson said it was too sweeping to claim that in asking all religious venues to be registered, house churches would, in effect, be outlawed. "On the contrary, the regulation will protect a large number of such meeting points by giving them a legal status."

Membership

Chinese Christians include people of all ages, in the city and in the country, in all walks of life. They have increased most rapidly in rural areas, where economic disruption has been greatest. Many new converts have been motivated by a healing experience. Church leaders recognize that prayers for the sick and home visits with blessings are legitimate expressions of faith but see miraculous healings as suspicious.

According to the Rev. Cao Shengjie, a vice president of the CCC, 70 percent of all believers are women. Jiang Peifen notes that "Today there are more women than men in church because women get in touch with their friends and bring them to church." Many of these older women have been Christians most of their lives. They tend to be conservative and resistant to change. But change is coming as younger people join.

One example of a church congregation being slowly changed by a growing presence of young people is the Shanghai West (Huxi) Church, built in 1989 in the Zhabei district. The district was once a poor industrial area but is undergoing rapid growth—marked by construction of shops and new apartment blocks (resulting in the relocation of many senior citizens), as well as increased vehicular traffic. Teachers, doctors, engineers, and business people are joining the congregation. Worship has taken on a new flavor as young people lead in hymn singing and conduct fellowships and Bible studies.

Women the majority of church members

This all marks something of a challenge for the older members of the congregation. The Rev. Sang Yuhan and Gan Xianzhen, church committee chairwoman, have encouraged older members to make new acquaintances, reminding them that it "it takes time and energy to understand others and to let them understand you."

In addition to the members of registered churches and meeting points and those who worship in their own homes, there are many followers of itinerant, self-proclaimed evangelists who meet in unregistered places. The government regards such behavior as "abnormal" and does not protect it. These self-styled evangelists are quite different from evangelists in more organized congregations. Some take advantage of their followers. RAB officials report disturbing incidents of cheating by these "bad elements." Some sell "miraculous" healing services for money, which is illegal. One such evangelist, Hua Xuehe from Huaiyin, collected enough money from 10 meeting points to build himself a new home. Bearing a name resembling the Chinese word for God in the Old Testament, he claimed to be a direct descendant of Jehovah.

To control these itinerant, self-styled evangelists, the government has enacted the "three designates" policy (designated preacher, area, and meeting place), which means that preaching and worship are to take place in designated areas and locations.

Worship

The focus of Christian life in China is the worship service. (Sunday schools have been developing in city churches. There was also a growing number of church-sponsored clinics, homes for the elderly, and social-service centers, but they were subordinate to worship.) Because churches and meeting points are few in relation to the number of believers, especially in rural areas, many people must travel long hours to attend, and services are usually crowded. The buildings may be Western-style churches inherited from the missionary era, such as most Roman Catholic cathedrals, or newly built functional structures. Meeting points are more numerous and tend to be simple and functional. For example, in Jiangsu Province there are more than 350 churches but more than 1,000 meeting points, ranging from 20 to 2,000 members.

Services range from an elaborate Catholic mass to a simple Protestant service of sharing testimonies, singing, and prayer. Pastors and lay leaders try to plan a worship environment that is welcoming to strangers. In rural areas these newcomers, who usually discover the congregation through curiosity or the invitation of a co-worker, have no other way but the service to learn about Christianity. (In urban areas there are

Overflow crowd in courtyard of Qingpu church, near Shanghai

religious bookshops, libraries, and church events on television.) The sermon must inform them about the faith, since they have little or no knowledge of it or are filled with misinformation and superstition. At the same time it must inspire them and help believers reach a deeper level of spiritual growth and commitment. Therefore, sermons tend to be long, lasting over an hour. The theology is generally conservative and tends to lean in the direction of fundamentalism and biblical literalism.

Since Bibles are in short supply and many seekers are illiterate, hymns are an important way to reach the congregation. Indigenous hymns reflecting the church's independence from the West are especially appealing. Many Christians have testified that they were drawn into the church when they heard people singing indigenous hymns.

Among Protestants, "a denominational mind may remain with some older Christians," said one pastor. "But in practice, churches pursue a very ecumenical course in observing Christian ordinances. For example, in observing communion, a church may follow a different tradition from week to week. The choice between sprinkling or immersion for baptism is often left to the individual. In colder months, when hot water is in short supply, sprinkling is clearly preferred."

Preference was the rule in an unusually large baptism service in Yangzhou in 1991, when 130 believers from surrounding areas without pastors were baptized in a city church. *Church Order for Trial Use* (1987) offers guidelines for local churches to develop their own regulations.

Services of worship conducted by the self-styled evangelists are quite different from those of CCC-aligned churches. Groups in the countryside that shout, speak in tongues, and shake their bodies when praying insist

Hymn-singing in Han church

that these actions show one is possessed by the Holy Spirit. Others tell that if they use a hymnal or worship on Sunday, they won't be saved. Still others say that those Christians who claim to be self-administering, self-supporting, and self-propagating (following the TSPM principles) won't be saved. In response, said one elderly pastor, "We tell them that Three-Self is not our faith. Our faith is in God and Jesus. We rely on the Bible for guidance and the Three-Self is for running the church well."

Leadership

The responsibility of leading the Chinese churches rests primarily with ordained clergy, but because there is a great shortage of them (only 1,500 to serve about 9,500 churches), lay evangelists and other workers play an important role. Most of the 30,000 odd meeting points are led by lay people, including many women. Most meeting points are linked to churches, which send out pastors to administer the sacraments. It may take months for the few pastors of a particular region to visit all the congregations. Rev. Lin De'en of Jiangsu Province said, "In one day I traveled many miles by bicycle baptizing a total of 700 people. Time was so short I had to eat while on the bicycle riding to the next place where many more were waiting."

Krystin Granberg

Clergyman baptizing a convert

The Witness of the Laity

The city of Wenzhou, on the southeast coast of Zhejing Province, has more than 400,000 Christians, who meet in more than 1,500 churches and meeting points. But there are only 133 full-time clergy and church workers to serve them. A great deal depends on the 3,000 lay men and women now serving as volunteer workers. Some contribute up to 40 hours a week to the life of the church. They are the mainstay, teaching Bible classes, organizing meetings, doing construction, and managing. "There is no way we carry on without their witness," commented a Wenzhou pastor.

"Without committed lay leaders," said Han Wenzao, acting general secretary of the CCC since 1994, "our churches wouldn't function, especially in the countryside. Our church is a lay person's church and we lay people have an important role to play in making our Christian presence felt in China."

In rural areas newly ordained seminary graduates are serving alongside aging pastors, who work tirelessly without thought of retirement. In some cases, the older pastors rejoice in enabling the younger generation to minister. But in other cases, older pastors struggle with them and even resist letting go and sharing responsibility—passing on the mantle—partly because they missed out on years of ministry during the difficult years of the Cultural Revolution.

The Leadership Gap

This conflict exposes one of the difficulties facing the church in China, a serious leadership gap caused by the forced closure of seminaries during the Cultural Revolution. That resulted in what some have called a "missing generation" of church leadership. The politics of seniority still hold fast. Of the 1,300 seminary graduates in China between 1985 and 1991—95 percent of whom work in local churches—fewer than 75 had been ordained by their church councils in the last 10 years. The year 1992 marked something of a milestone in reversing the "graying" of the Chinese church leadership. On 6 January the Fifth National Christian Conference, as part of the general theme "Running the Church Well," called for an emphasis on younger leadership and held an unprecedented event: the ordination of 45 new pastors, 17 of them women.

Han Wenzao said the church must prepare and promote the younger generation for positions of leadership. "There are several younger people in positions where they can gain experience, and I hope that they will be elected into leadership positions at the next National Christian Conference in 1996." Han emphasized that reducing the responsibilities of older pastors to make room for those younger does not mean "sacking" the older generation or diminishing their roles in the church. In fact, the emergence of new leaders in the church is a credit to those who have served so faithfully for so long. A new generation, which will in due time find it just as difficult to pass the mantle to its successors, has a big enough task ahead without facing resistance.

"In the next two years it will become apparent which younger people are best suited, inspired, and committed to serve as leaders in this crucial juncture in the history of the church in China. More young church leaders will be drawn from all parts of the country as well as Shanghai and Nanjing," said Han. Recognizing that now is the time for new and

EFFECTS OF THE CULTURAL REVOLUTION ON TWO CHURCH LEADERS

To understand the effects of the Cultural Revolution on two generations of China's church leadership, the experiences of Dr. Han Wenzao, acting general secretary of the CCC, and the Rev. Bao Jiayuan, associate general secretary of the CCC, are instructive.

Han, born in Shanghai in 1923 into a non-Christian family, became actively involved in the church while attending Hangzhou Christian College. Trained as an engineer, he devoted much of his time during and after World War II to student relief work and in the late 1940s helped organize the Nanjing Christian Council, as the well as the TSPM. In 1961 he took charge of the administration of Nanjing Union Theological Seminary—shifting, he said, from civil engineering to "human engineering." Han learned something of the complexities of that task during the Cultural Revolution, when Red Guards threatened to destroy the seminary's library. With courage and ingenuity he confronted them and with a colleague saved the best 10 percent of the collection. He also managed to keep a pocket-size New Testament with Psalms for his daily use. When the seminary staff and faculty were forced to work in the fields, Han learned about the needs of Christians in rural areas. Today, that is the basis for his efforts to improve church work in the countryside.

Bao was born in Suzhou in 1944 into a family that had been Christian for generations. The son of a minister and evangelist, He entered Nanjing Union Theological Seminary in 1962, at a time of decline for the church. Only 19 students were enrolled when he graduated in 1966, shortly before the Cultural Revolution. As all churches were closed, Bao had no chance to serve as a minister. The family home was ransacked and his father's extensive library burned; Bao's father was held by the Red Guards; and Bao had to work as a tailor while taking care of his bed-ridden mother. Eventually the family was reunited, but they were sent to a very poor area in northern Jiangsu, where they had no contact with other Christians. Still, they managed to worship together using an English-language Bible In 1976 the family returned to Suzhou, where they continued their family worship services. Meanwhile, Bao worked as an electrician, a tour guide, and an interpreter for a Chinese construction project in Kuwait. Rreturning to China to work for the TSPM, he was finally ordained in 1988—a full 22 years after graduating from seminary!

renewed ministry by Chinese Christians, Han said he and others would be working to ensure the church benefits from the new generation.

Training and Supporting New Leaders

The ordained Protestant clergy have been educated in a system that now includes 13 theological training centers, located in the provinces of Jiangsu, Anhui, Fujian, Guangdong, Liaoning, Sichuan, Zhejiang, Hubei, Shandong, Shanxi, and Yunnan, as well as the municipalities of Beijing and Shanghai with four-year or two-year programs. The most outstanding is the national one, Nanjing Union Theological Seminary. They have a total enrollment of about 850 and graduate an average of 200 a year. The CCC's Commission on Theological Education works to improve the quality of seminaries and sets standards of curriculum, libraries, teaching staff, and student accommodations.

Nanjing Seminary graduated its 10th class in 1994. There were 43 graduates from different programs. From 1985 to 1993, the seminary graduated 463 students, of whom 415 are now working in the church. About 60 Nanjing graduates teach in seminaries all over China.

Sichuan Seminary, which serves the southwest, celebrated its 10th anniversary in September 1994. Graduates have included members of regional ethnic minority groups. In the first eight years there were 120 graduates. The fourth class meets in the new seven-story building, a big improvement over the borrowed space of the local church in Chengdu where the seminary had its beginning.

The Rev. Su Deci, principal of Huadong (East China) Seminary in Shanghai, points out that "Theological training has become more critical and a campus 15 times bigger must be found to make it possible for more students to receive theological training, including Christian art and music." As chair of the CCC Theological Education Commission, he works for the day when all theological training centers will be able to accommodate more people who are willing to serve.

New graduates must be strongly motivated by faith, because funds for their support are low. Older pastors, who were forced into "productive work" during the Cultural Revolution, generally have pensions from their secular jobs to support them. But young pastors must be fully recompensed by their congregations. In most cases their salaries are a financial headache for the congregation, especially in rural areas.

The Rev. Zheng Yugui, president of the Fujian Christian Council and Fugian Theological Seminary, said that some theology graduates earn the equivalent of U.S. $35 a month, but others working in poor mountainous areas often make the equivalent of only U.S. $3.50 to $6.00, not enough to live on. The CCC has set up a fund to subsidize the salaries of church workers in poor areas and provide for their theological training.

The pastor of a church in Shandong, a graduate of a training course for evangelists at Nanjing Seminary, has personal experience of financial pressure.

Our church has its origin in the Jesus Family and we are used to mutual support on a very personal basis. The believers can't afford to pay me a salary. Instead the brothers and sisters do most of my farm work on the share of farmland I get under the pubic contract system and lend a hand at home. This frees my wife and me for the work of the church.

Recognizing the need to train rural lay workers, in 1987 Nanjing Seminary set up a pilot program under Elder Sister Jiang Peifen. Many regional and provincial seminaries have since established one-year programs.

In addition, Nanjing offers a three-year theological correspondence course, which enrolls about 4,000 students. County or local church councils sponsor hundreds of three-week to six-month training classes for rural church leaders. On a less structured basis, the CCC publishes a syllabus to inform grass-roots church workers of resources such as Bible studies, sermon ideas, and devotional material. It has 45,000 subscribers.

Running the Church Well

One of the principal challenges and worries facing church leaders is that of "running the church well," particularly the grass-roots churches. Many of them, in Bishop Ting's own words, "are in a mess" and "are very poorly run."

In a November 1994 meeting of the China Christian Council and the Three-Self Patriotic Movement, Ting said these two national Christian bodies receive letters daily from local churches, "and many are tales of woe from believers: what a tyrant their pastor is—what he says goes, he consults with no one, the accounts are not public, and donations disappear, . . . the congregation has no say, and the church council never holds elections, etc., etc." As a result, many Christians are refusing to attend church and congregate elsewhere. "This is splitting the church, destroying its unity, and it is a very serious matter indeed."

Resolving this problem, according to Ting, will require a reemphasis on democratizing the church—that decisions be made in consultation among church members themselves. There is, he noted, a strong democratic tradition within the church:

The Christian Church in the first century worked through its difficulties through forms of a democratic process. In mirroring the early church, the church

Many women in a class at East China Theological Seminary

in China will be able to foster a more democratic process, so that leaders of the grass-roots church can be made accountable to their Christian sisters and brothers.

In Buddhism a temple is opened and the believers themselves go to burn incense and worship Buddha. Protestantism and Catholicism are much more organized. A church has its church council. . . . To run our grass-roots churches well, grass-roots organization must play its part. We must act with a democratic spirit . . . with everything done through consultation. Contact must be maintained, discussion fostered, and things done publicly. Consultation does not end with soliciting opinions, even less is it a matter of "I talk and you listen." Consultation is a sincere exchange of views, contact, and study, involving everyone. Consultation is the tradition of the church, whether it is a church with an episcopal system, a presbyterian system, or a congregational system. Consultation is indispensable to all of them and should be even more so for us. Only through consultation can the internal problems of grass-roots churches and meeting points be solved. The national level must consult with the provincial, the provincial with the municipal, the municipal with the county, and the county with the grass roots. In this way, believers will be happier. They will feel they have a say in things. It's not for us to remove a pastor the congregation has problems with. We have no authority to remove someone. It must be solved through consultation at the grass roots.

The Witness of Women

Women, who make up the majority of Christians in China, play an indispensable role in church renewal and Christian service in the community. In reflecting on their work in the church, the Rev. Cao Shengjie acknowledges that God gives women talent that should not be blotted out or looked down on. Outstanding women such as Cora Deng, Wu Yifang, and Jiang Peifen were in the forefront of the YWCA, the TSPM, and Christian education at the policy-making level. On a less exalted plane, women have been active in schools for Bible studies and preparation for preaching since the 19th century, when a women's Bible school was founded in Ningbo in 1844. Since then, increasing numbers of schools at all levels from primary to seminary have produced many church professionals. In 1995 over 56 percent of students in the 13 theological seminaries were women, and about 14 percent of the clergy were women, enormous progress since 1949.

WITNESS WITHOUT WORDS

One of the outstanding Christian women to come through the journey of postwar Christianity was the distinguished educator Wu Yifang (1893-1985). At a time when few Chinese women went to school, she graduated from Jinling College in Nanjing, then a mission school founded in 1912, and later became its president. She was a minister of education for Jiangsu Province and represented China at the founding of the United Nations in San Francisco in 1945. She represented the educational sector at the National Chinese People's Political Consultative Conference, which helped shape the Constitution of 1982. She served on the conference presidium with other Protestants, Catholics, and Buddhists. When confined to a hospital in her late years, she kept taking "leaves of absence" so that she could go on attending meetings. She was deeply loved. At a memorial service after her death in 1985 at age 93, she was given the following tribute:

When we speak about witness, we do not limit it to the narrow definition of mouthing the name of Jesus as savior to those who are not believers. Though it is not good to refrain from speaking when it is time to speak, the witness without words is also a witness, which is acceptable to the Lord. To work for a good constitution, to participate in bringing justice to one's country, to improve the image of the church and bring it closer to the people in order that people are more willing to listen to the gospel offered by the church—all these are the nature of proclaiming the gospel, because these are preparing the way of the Lord. We can learn much about this from the life of Wu Yifang. Many who shed tears did not know the Christ of the first chapter of John as she knew him. But Christ had influence on them through the life of Wu Yifang.

A film was made of Wu Yifang's life to be shown on television in fall 1995. An Amity teacher from California plays Miss Matilda Thurston, the founder of Jinling and Wu's teacher.[6]

Nevertheless, Cao points out that 90 percent of church women surveyed by the CCC before the Fourth UN Conference on Women in 1995 thought women were not sufficiently valued in the church; they lack opportunities to participate in policy making and are seldom allowed to preach or lead the service on special occasions.

The Rev. Gao Ying, a pastor of Chong Wenen Church in Beijing, confirms this judgment.

Women's liberation has had a strong impact on the church. Before the founding of the People's Republic of China, few women were ministers, but now there are many women ministers. Since 1979 the church in China has ordained more than 400 pastors, of whom more than 60 are women. At present one of every ten people receiving ordination is a woman. Most women seminarians expect some day to be ordained.

Women leaving Qini church in the Guandong countryside to work in the fields

Women are vital in the life and work of the Chinese church. Today more than half of the believers are women. In my church women make up more than 60 percent of the congregation and most of them are very involved in congregational activities, from cleaning the church, acting as ushers and visiting to singing in the choir and preparing communion. But the hands that prepare the communion are not allowed to distribute it at the communion service on Sunday. They make the bread and prepare the grape juice, they set the Eucharistic table, and they clean the cups and plates afterwards, but such participation is only behind the scenes.

Three years ago, upon my return to Beijing after studying in the United States, I was startled to see only white-haired men standing at the front of the church receiving the consecrated elements from the pastor before distributing them to the congregation. The striking contrast between what I saw in Western churches and the reality I faced in my Beijing church was shocking.

Even I, as a pastor, was not allowed to officiate at communion. I waited patiently. I never gave up the struggle. Finally, one day I was asked to replace a sick pastor and officiate at the Eucharist at the Saturday evening worship. It was the first time that a woman led the Eucharist in my church. It was also the first time I had officiated at communion since being ordained. Although Saturday evening worship is much smaller than Sunday morning worship, with around 400 worshipers, my participation was a breakthrough and a genuine step towards gender equality. It took another six months before I officiated at Eucharist on Sunday.

We Christian women of China must make liberation our own struggle. Women's emancipation is an ongoing process, and we have a long way to go before achieving greater leadership participation and partnership equality.

The church in China, ruled primarily by an older generation of male leadership, seems unready to accept the changes that will thrust it ahead of encrusted cultural attitudes. Women's full liberation and independence can be achieved only when men, as well as women, experience a mental shift from the traditional religious values to modern biblical concepts. Chinese women in particular have a long struggle ahead before we are allowed, as Mao Zedong said, to hold up half the sky.[7]

In addition to their professional problems, Chinese women clergy face the challenge of balancing their professional life with the social and economic demands on them. The Rev. Chen Tingting, who was ordained in 1992, one of the first women pastors in Zhejiang Province, says,

Having chosen to do church work as my profession does not mean I can give up farming. Nor can I neglect my duties at home as a filial daughter-in-law, a traditional wife and a mother. I am responsible to lead three congregations and many church meetings take place in the evenings in addition to Bible studies.

Of course serving God in rural China is not all smooth sailing. While preaching is one of my main tasks, it is more important to live it. We young church workers are constantly reminded not to let others despise us because of our youth. We are a witness to Christ not only within the church but in our society at large as well. This year my family received a "model family" award in our village. This too is our way of witness in Socialist China—that Christians are good examples and good citizens demonstrating God's love in all that we do.[8]

Without the devoted efforts of lay women, local churches would find it difficult to exist. Cao notes that in local churches women's fellowships work hard to spread the gospel. They do so partly by holding prayer meetings, Bible studies, witnessing sessions, and conferences. One important aspect of their effort is teaching women to read. (Some 100 million women in China are illiterate.) They also witness to their faith by undertaking more practical tasks such as cleaning and decorating the church, mending Bibles and hymnals, sewing clothes and mending toys for needy families, holding charity bazaars, raising funds for flood relief, and providing health education and first aid. Extending their influence, Christian women in Chengdu have formed a Christian Women's Service Committee to organize and coordinate their work in children's welfare, health care, literacy campaigns, and other issues related to the position of women in society.

Waiting for a computer class to start at the YWCA/YMCA in Shanghai

Youth in a Modern Money Economy

The church in China, like the church anywhere else, must pay particular attention to attracting young people if it is to continue and flourish. That is not easy in a society that is overwhelmingly secular and in the last 20 years has been increasingly concerned with money and what it can buy. According to a church leader writing in 1987:

Today's youth are tasting the benefits of an economy oriented toward production of consumer goods. They feel the freedom of being able to set up independent enterprises rather than being tied to jobs assigned to them by the government. Many have been able to form impressions about the outside world and travel abroad. And many are receiving a better education. Along with this has

The streets of China today are less likely to be lined with market stalls and dumpling shops than with signs advertising American cigarettes. The World Health Organization warns that "In the next century approximately 50 million mainland Chinese youth under the age of 20 will die a premature death from illnesses related to smoking, a grim reminder of the destructive and wasteful ways in which young people are being enticed to spend their money."

come [a] commensurate rise in expectations. As in other countries, Chinese youth today have more than their elders had, and they want and expect more. As a result they are not satisfied with the pace of modernization and reform. It is too slow for them and frustrating. The ongoing interplay of expectations and opportunities will have a major impact upon this youth generation and the society at large. The motivation and involvement of this significant part of China's population in the country's development will largely determine how their expectations are addressed. The outcome will be either a terrible setback and disappointment or a powerful incentive for a generation of young people with the desire and motivation to build New China.

Church leaders and academics meeting at the Christianity and Modernization Conference in Beijing in 1994 expressed concern about youth. "Many young people stop going to church because of conflicts they feel," said Sun Li of the Institute of Religious Studies in Shanghai.

At work young business people are required to be productive and make money, not only for themselves but for their company. But clergy and elders give them the impression that they should never advocate material profit. They believe that religion expresses its holy image through transcendence of this material world as "money is the root of all evil" in religion, and purity and poverty are conditions of salvation of the soul.

Taking into account the tendency of many elderly Christians to reject this world in favor of the next, Sun pondered how young Christians could possibly discuss their problems in their business-oriented and moneymaking lives. "The gap created causes some young people to go to church less or to stop going altogether," he concluded.

According to the late Bishop Shen Yifan,

It is important for Chinese theological thought to absorb the best of Chinese traditional culture. But more important is the way in which Chinese theological thought should respond to the tremendous political, social, economic, and cultural changes that have taken place in contemporary China. Are material progress and human accomplishments works of Satan which lead people away from God, or do they reveal the wisdom and compassion of God as they come to be enjoyed by all people?

CHRISTIAN YOUTH CLEAN SMELLY CREEK

In the coastal area of Fujian Province is a village with a small creek running through it. Used for drainage of rain and domestic waste water, no one paid much attention to it. But with industrialization and growth of the village, the creek filled up with all sorts of rubbish and waste and became smelly. A threat to the environment, it became the village's sorrow.

There were a number of Christians in the village. All these years they had taken it as their duty to help the aged, the sick, and the needy and to bring comfort to the bereaved and the unfortunate, Christian and non-Christian alike. Their work brought many, including young folk, to Christ, and the Christian community grew year after year.

Eager to participate, about 100 of the Christian youths got together to rid the village of the health hazard. They spent three days and nights cleaning up the creek. They lined the bottom of it with bricks purchased with their own money. The effect was stupendous—the whole village was shocked. Many villagers told the Christian elders that Christians are indeed the cream of the land. The Party Secretary of the village confided to the leaders that formerly he was worried to see so many young people become Christians. Having witnessed what they had done in the past, however, and seeing how they voluntarily and quickly cleaned up the creek, he said he would feel at ease to hear of any conversions in the future, for Christians had proved themselves worthy [citizens].[9]

Should the younger generation reject material life and give up all efforts for human improvement in this world in order to draw closer to God? Or should they enter into the real world, and work toward the improvement of material and cultural life so that they may come closer to the will of God?

Zeng Qingyun spoke on a Christian's attitude to money, a subject of particular relevance to the young as they start new careers.

Having money in China is something new. Christianity does not necessarily imply impoverishment and scarcity. Theological trends towards asceticism and ideas that greater poverty implies greater spirituality have been historically proven to be harmful. The true Christian relies on God's grace and proper, legal, diligent and fair means of production and management for his or her wealth and does not gain wealth by corruption and serving mammon.

We hear the expression "the love of money is the root of all evil," yet the social trend is that everything is focused around money and money is the ultimate. Frenzied worship of money has almost driven people mad as they try to get money by means of corruption, bribery, smuggling, tax evasion, pirating goods and pornography. The true Christian will not follow this trend and get contaminated.

The spiritual implication of grace and blessings is no longer personal gain or personal acceptance, but is the sacrifice and giving which Christ's love impels. Chinese believers must be encouraged to cast off the ideological means. Many believers have become skilled trades persons, and entrepreneurs contributing to the prosperity of the Chinese economy.

Given the many difficulties undergone by the Christian church in China through its long history, it is not surprising that its tremendous growth since 1979 has been hailed as a triumph of the spirit. At the same time, it continues to face problems both within and without, and it will remain a minority religion in a country of 1.2 billion. The question facing Christians in China is no longer "Whither the church?" but rather "What faithful role can we play?" It is not a question that yields easy answers.

---

1. Edmund Doogue, "Inside China," *One World*, July 1944, p. 12.
2. Gail Coulson, "New Steps Toward Protection of Religion in China," *China Talk*, August 1994
3. Doogue, "Inside China."
4. Doogue, "Inside China."
5. Doogue, "Inside China."
6. *China News Update* July 1986 and September 1995.
7. Excerpts from Gao Ying's article in *In God's Image*, spring 1994, published by the Asia Women's Resource Center for Culture and Theology in Seoul, and adapted in *One World*, July 1994.
8. *China News Update*, July 1991.
9. Adapted from Zhang Guangzhou, "Living as Christians Today," *Chinese Theological Review*, 1988, pp. 55-68.

Chapter 3

Hong Kong and
Its Churches

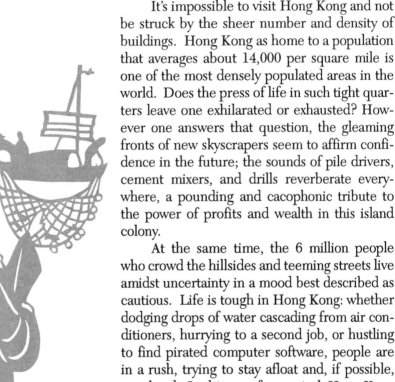

It's impossible to visit Hong Kong and not be struck by the sheer number and density of buildings. Hong Kong as home to a population that averages about 14,000 per square mile is one of the most densely populated areas in the world. Does the press of life in such tight quarters leave one exhilarated or exhausted? However one answers that question, the gleaming fronts of new skyscrapers seem to affirm confidence in the future; the sounds of pile drivers, cement mixers, and drills reverberate everywhere, a pounding and cacophonic tribute to the power of profits and wealth in this island colony.

At the same time, the 6 million people who crowd the hillsides and teeming streets live amidst uncertainty in a mood best described as cautious. Life is tough in Hong Kong: whether dodging drops of water cascading from air conditioners, hurrying to a second job, or hustling to find pirated computer software, people are in a rush, trying to stay afloat and, if possible, get ahead. In this race for survival, Hong Kong was rated the most stressful city in the world in 1994. It claims other distinctions, too: Hong Kong has more cellular phones per capita than anywhere else and more cellular phones than cars. When dating, it is not unusual for young adults to give a partner a cellular phone. When

High-rise buildings and signs of Western food shops on a Hong Kong street

you live and work in confined places, it is an indispensable way to talk in private.

As one of the world's greatest financial and service centers—rivaling New York and Tokyo—a city that long ago left behind the image of a settlement of fisher folk, Hong Kong faces a peculiar challenge unknown to other international capitals: on 1 July 1997 the 156-year-old British colony will become the Hong Kong Special Administrative Region (HKSAR) of the People's Republic of China.

Long, strenuous, and often bitter negotiations between China and Britain have led many of the territory's residents, trusting neither sovereign power, to act in their own interests. Many Hong Kong residents, formerly refugees from China, fear control from the country they fled, particularly during a time when China will soon face the question of who will succeed the increasingly infirm Deng Xiaoping. Political developments are considered more unpredictable than social and economic ones, and there is fear and anticipation as July 1997 nears.

Two years before the event, Hong Kong's hotels were already solidly booked for 1 July 1997, primarily by the international news media. It is expected to be a mega-media event, with dignitaries and fireworks in abundance. Ocean liners may have to be brought in to provide extra rooms for all the visitors from China and abroad.

With the lowering of the Union Jack, the last British governor of Hong Kong will exit. A new chief executive, invested with authority by China, will take up the new appointment as flags of the People's Republic of China and the HKSAR are hoisted at midnight. Whoever takes office will face a region of many different peoples, cultures, and religions. It is not yet clear who, and who will not, be celebrating.

A Variety of People

Hong Kong's population is 98 percent Chinese, but there are also residents from Southeast Asia, the Philippines, and the Western world. Some foreign visitors find Hong Kong's variety stimulating and its energy contagious as they flow easily with the hurried day-to-day surge of the colony. As one visitor from Africa said, "Everyone is doing something, and I wish people in my country could be here to feel the enterprising spirit." Other visitors see nothing but a mass of stolid faces hurrying by—and when the summer humidity presses down, it can seem as if the high rises are almost squeezing the breath out of the city. Hong Kong still feels over-crowded, even though the colony's birth rate is one of the lowest in Asia and the median age is in the early 30s—up from the mid-20s in 1982.

Chinese Immigrants Old and New

Hong Kong is a community of immigrants; some have been there for generations, some have just arrived. Chinese make up 98 percent of the population, but they come from numerous regions in China. The largest number are Cantonese from neighboring Guandong Province. Cantonese began to settle in Hong Kong about 100 B.C. Another group of old-time immigrants over a period of a thousand years are the Hakka, the descendants of Han Chinese who migrated south in times of flood, famine, or turmoil in the north. Other groups came in the 17th century. Still others came from Shanghai, from the provinces of Fuzhou, Jiangsu, and Zhejiang, and from Taiwan.

Now immigrants arrive daily from China. In the 1990s Hong Kong permitted about 38,000 immigrants from China to settle in the colony each year. In 1995 daily one-way permits for immigrants from the mainland increased from 105 to 150, 30 of them reserved for children. This 43 percent increase in the immigration quota unites many families who have endured border separations, with one parent usually a Hong Kong resident. The system has been designed to prevent a sudden influx of those entitled to enter after 1 July 1997.

Even so, current social and education resources are insufficient to cope with these arrivals. Newly arrived immigrant children face a shortage of schools and many have been forced to return to the mainland to continue their education, especially when they lack English skills or are overage and are not accepted by local schools. There are other problems, too: young people have to adjust to a life that is far more harried and crowded than it is in the mainland.

A growing group of recent and new arrivals are Chinese who emigrated after 1984 and have returned for cultural and financial reasons—opportunities abroad do not always meet expectations. They have returned to take advantage of the region's exceptional economic growth. The Rev. Li Ping-Kwong, former president of the Methodist Church, Hong Kong, has pointed out that those who leave were often urged to do so by parents or other family members with bad experiences in China. "The children's future welfare is made a concern," he said, "but for those of us born in Hong Kong, there is always the compulsion to come back."

Contract Workers and Expatriate Personnel

In addition to its citizens, Hong Kong has a number of foreigners who are there on a temporary basis. There were about 200,000 in 1994. At the bottom of the labor force are migrant workers from China who work under contract. Since Hong Kong's shift from a manufacturing to a service economy, there has been greater demand for high-level skills. Because Hong Kong's citizens are increasingly well educated to take skilled jobs, they avoid low-skilled jobs—the so-called 3-D jobs (dangerous, demanding, and dirty). These must be done by outside help. Many work visas go to contract workers from China. Although they are paid less than Hong Kong residents, their salaries are still higher than they would be in China. Similarly, as more Hong Kong women work at skilled jobs, imported household help is more common. About 140,000 foreign workers were household workers, all but 10,000 or so from the Philippines.

Ranking above migrant workers in the labor force are members of the foreign, or expatriate, community. This small but varied group includes professional workers, business people, journalists, educators, employees of nongovernmental agencies, church workers, and British government personnel. In addition to Britain, these foreign workers hail from India, Pakistan, Singapore, the Philippines, Japan, the United States, Canada, Australia, New Zealand, Portugal, Sir Lanka, and nearby Macao. There is also a group of "stateless" people awaiting immigration decisions.

One of the largest expatriate communities in Hong Kong are Canadians, because Canada has forged a robust trading relationship with China. Canada was one of the first countries to sell wheat to the Chinese government. Nearly 30,000 Hong Kong residents hail from the United

States. They include North Americans of Chinese descent, Western-educated Hong Kong Chinese returning home, first-generation Vietnamese Americans, and others. Given the slowdown of the U.S. economy in the 1990s, these workers don't ask for, or receive, the high salaries and perks that formerly were necessary to lure them to Hong Kong.

Hong Kong has always attracted foreigners seeking adventure and fortune. Recently this appeal has become a problem for the colony, as young Britons, faced with high unemployment rates in their own country, have come in larger numbers to make quick money, usually in legitimate business, sometimes in the trading of illegal drugs, smuggling, fraud, prostitution, and theft. Keen to cash in on the closing days of the colony, they have taken advantage of their eligibility for work permits. Hong Kong police report that the increase of crime in the foreign community has coincided with the influx of these younger people, and that hundreds in their 20s and 30s have engaged in such criminal activity. The drug dealing is particularly bothersome. Bringing drugs with them from England, the young people have sold them for double the price in Hong Kong.

Still, the picture is not all of crime: many expatriates are hard workers and find Hong Kong's energy contagious. The optimism has been tempered in recent years, however, as the economy of the 1990s has flattened in comparison with the boom years of 1975 to 1989. Corporate cutbacks have become more common, and creeping insecurity has set in. For many people, earning enough to pay the rent has become the sole purpose for living.

Even so, many remain optimistic about the immense economic potential of the growing Asia Pacific region. Many also enjoy living in a truly international city. New generations of foreigners in Hong Kong are less likely to live in separate enclaves of familiar cultural conformity. The effort to reach out across cultural and language barriers is no longer considered novel. Still, there are those who leave Hong Kong a quarter century after arriving without having learned to say "thank you" or "excuse me" in Chinese.

The Flight of the Middle Class

Hong Kong has long been a point of transience. Not only are there waves of immigration, there are also cycles of departure as citizens emigrate for better opportunities abroad and expatriates, such as British civil servants, return home. The exodus that has been going on since the late 1980s is partly in anxiety about of the end of British rule and partly the effect of the increasing strength of China's economy. At the beginning of this period, 20,000 people a year were returning to China. Some were retirees, and others had been management and staff of factories relocated on the mainland or of joint economic ventures. A few thousand have been going to Taiwan each year—7,000 in 1990.

The departure of large numbers of technical personnel and highly skilled middle managers and professionals for Australia, Canada, and the United States is referred to as the "brain drain"—as if those remaining in Hong Kong lack brains or potential! Still, this high labor turnover and job hopping has created a loss of efficiency, and packages of high salaries and other benefits offered to encourage workers to stay on in Hong Kong have added to inflation. The departure of some community leaders and an alarming number of pastors has been a social loss.

In the mid-1980s, some 20,000 people a year were emigrating over-seas. In 1989, 42,000 left, increasing to 62,000 as confidence was shaken by the 1989 Tiananmen Square crackdown. Emigration peaked in 1992 at 66,000 and dropped to 54,000 by 1993. Canada alone received 42,000 new immigrants from Hong Kong the following year, making Chinese the third largest language group in Canada after English and French.

What do these figures mean? Do they mean that all people leaving had no faith in the future of Hong Kong? Or had they merely grown tired of the crowded and tense life Hong Kong offers?

As the Rev. Lincoln Leung, president of the Methodist Church, Hong Kong, explained:

When I came from Shanghai in 1948, it was supposed to be temporary. I thought we would return, but we didn't go back. Many like me have known the rootlessness. Hong Kong was not supposed to be a permanent place. If there could be no return, many dispersed to Western and Asian countries. Some who had the means established themselves in business. Now they leave for other countries because fears remain with them. My family may be in Canada but they understand that I have strong feelings to remain in Hong Kong and serve the church.

The second and third generations, however, do not necessarily have the same problem of rootlessness, as Katherine Ng, a church executive secretary, explained:

I was born, grew up, and was educated here. I gained much from Hong Kong and its people and want to put back. My attitude has been to be educated, work hard, and get promoted so as to better serve Hong Kong.

Part of Ng's commitment to Hong Kong stems from a 1991 campaign organized by the Hong Kong Christian Council called "We Love Hong Kong," which helped redirect attention from those leaving Hong Kong to those staying.

After all, I was brought up in Hong Kong, it is my home and I could take responsibility and contribute to society as it had contributed to me. With the training I received I wanted to continue to serve the community, to appreciate and celebrate the industrious character of our people, and, in turn, encourage them to carry on.

In recent years, then, Hong Kong has become not only a lifeboat for transients, a migrant city where mainland Chinese sought temporary asylum and foreign traders found business opportunities, but a permanent home to its residents. Most of them will stay after 1997.

A Variety of Religions

When fed strong doses of Hong Kong villains and gangsters in the movies, many Westerners find it difficult to imagine communities of faith in Hong Kong. Protestant and Catholic Christians together comprise a little more than 8 percent of Hong Kong's population, a little more than 500,000 in all. They are a strong, distinct minority, but their faith does not prevent them from participating to some degree in traditional Chinese beliefs and practices.

Most Hong Kong Chinese, even Christians, have Daoist, Buddhist, and Confucian traditions in their blood as part of their cultural identity. They may accept the Daoist principle that a balance of the natural forces of yin and yang will achieve a harmonious existence. They may also strive for the ideal of compassion as taught by the Buddha. Most of them observe the traditional rules of filial piety and hierarchical family relationships that are stressed by Confucianism. Most of them venerate their ancestors, celebrate traditional holidays such as New Year, and mark weddings and funerals in traditional ways. Many continue such folkways as observing taboos to ward off evil spirits, lighting joss (luck) sticks of incense before an image of a god in a hall or place of business, and situating new buildings out of the paths of evil spirits. Although these practices are becoming less common, they are still much in evidence.

For non-Christian Chinese, there are no hard and fast lines between Buddhist and Daoist traditions. Daoist and Buddhist deities are often honored together in one temple. At the end of 1994, Buddhists from around the world gathered at the Po Lin Monastery on Hong Kong's Lantau Island to inaugurate the Tian Tan Buddha—the largest outdoor statue of Buddha in the world. They also honored the lotus flower, which is sacred to Buddhists as a symbol of purity and perfection since it originated in the mud and is able to preserve its purity, as Buddha did in his life on earth. The lotus also holds great significance for Daoists as the symbol of the Eight Immortals. The lotus appears in works of art, and its roots, petals, and seeds are used in Chinese cooking.

Mosque, Hong Kong

A small minority of Hong Kong people, about 50,000, are Muslims. More than half of these are Chinese; the rest are either non-Chinese born in Hong Kong or immigrants from Pakistan, India, Malaysia, Indonesia, the Middle East, and Africa. The oldest of the four principal mosques used daily for prayers is the Jamia Mosque, built in the late 19th century.

A still smaller minority—about 12,000—are Hindus. Their close-knit community is centered on the Hindu Temple in Happy Valley. The Hindu Association of Hong Kong is responsible for upkeep of the temple.

There are also Sikhs. They came to Hong Kong from Punjab in northern India as part of the British armed forces during the 19th century. They comprised a large segment of the Royal Hong Kong Police Force before World War II. The men are distinguished by a beard, an iron bracelet, and a turban hiding their uncut hair.

Roman Catholics

The Roman Catholic Church has been present in Hong Kong since the territory's earliest days. Established as a mission prefecture in 1841 and as an apostolic vicarate in 1874, Hong Kong became a diocese in 1946. In the 1990s the bishop was John Baptist Wu, who was consecrated in 1975 and made a cardinal in 1988. Nearly 250,000 Hong Kong residents (5 percent of the population) are Roman Catholic. With the large influx of household workers from the Philippines, the Catholic population has grown by 90,000 in recent years. The Catholic presence is felt throughout the territory, through churches, study centers, schools, and bookstores. Catholic health, medical, and social-service agencies are administrated under Caritas, which has also made outstanding contributions to development and relief work in China.

Protestants

In the 150 years since the first Protestant church was founded in Hong Kong, the Protestant community has grown to 258,000 in more than 900 congregations representing 52 denominations and independent churches. The Baptists are the largest denomination, followed by the Lutherans. Other major denominations include Adventists, Anglicans, the Christian Missionary Alliance, Methodists, Pentecostals, and Church of Christ in China (which is a union of Presbyterians, Congregationalists, and other traditions). The number of independent churches has increased significantly owing to the strong evangelical zeal of lay Christians.

In addition to playing a crucial role in the spiritual life of the territory, churches also play a key role in the civic culture of Hong Kong, whether in education, health, or social action. Protestant organizations assist in the operation of three university-level institutions: Chung Chi College at the Chinese University of Hong Kong, Hong Kong Baptist University, and Lingnan College. Protestants run 122 secondary schools, 141 primary schools, and 146 kindergartens, as well as 13 theological seminaries and Bible institutes, 16 Christian publishing houses, and 57 Christian book stores. Protestants are also deeply involved in health care, administering seven hospitals with more than 2,000 beds, 24 clinics, and 61 social-service organizations that provide a wide range of social services, including 108 community and youth centers, 35 child-care centers, 8 children's homes, 27 homes for the elderly, 78 centers for the elderly, 3 schools for the deaf,

Family fellowship in an Anglican parish

10 training centers for the mentally challenged, and 20 camp sites. Five international hotel-type guest houses and numerous programs for people of all ages are managed by the YMCA and YWCA.

Ninety-six parachurch agencies and various Christian action groups have been established as catalytic agents of renewal, to minister to the needs of the Protestant community and to respond to current issues and concerns in Hong Kong society at large. The church is involved in overseas aid by supporting emergency relief and development projects in developing countries. Two weekly newspapers, the *Christian Weekly* and the *Christian Times*, bring news and comments from a Christian perspective to the church community. Two interdenominational bodies facilitate cooperative work among Protestant churches—the Hong Kong Chinese Christian Churches Union, established in 1915, which has a membership of 259 congregations, and the Hong Kong Christian Council (HKCC), established in 1954, which has 19 member denominations, and organizations such as the YMCA and YWCA.

Reunification

Decolonization is never easy, but Hong Kong's case is uniquely challenging because it will not move to independence 1 July 1997 but will return to the sovereign power whence many of Hong Kong's residents or their families fled during times of turmoil. Hong Kong residents want their home to remain a vibrant, international city—a haven for personal rights and freedoms guaranteed by an accountable government. Whether China can afford to be that kind of government remains the unanswered question. In the meantime, people await a possibly difficult transition. Some have come to trust neither China nor Britain during the often bitter negotiations between the two countries. Some believe that Deng Xiaoping's "one country, two systems" policy was devised to prevent decolonization from Britain and instead create a form of recolonization by China. The fact is, Hong Kong residents have not been the ones determining their future—which is why the rallying cry of "Hong Kong people ruling Hong Kong" has become so popular.

"It's not a matter of authoritarianism versus democracy, but rather finding a balance between central authority and local autonomy," said the Rev. Peter Lee, former director of the Christian Study Centre for Culture and Religion. "The relationship will have to be one of mutual trust, a common national loyalty and respect for individuation of the region, and balance between the rule of law and humane qualities. There are ingredients in Chinese culture which lend themselves to a satisfactory solution to the problem, but the people concerned must work at it."

The Facts in Perspective

From 1842 on, the British secured an area of 412 square miles, including Hong Kong Island, the Kowloon peninsula, and adjacent New Territories, by three treaties that China considered unequal and invalid. Though the 1997 lease concerns only the New Territories, Britain realized it had to negotiate over the entire area. Hong Kong Island and Kowloon are dependent on the comparatively extensive New Territories for the colony's airport, water supply, electrical plant, and manufacturing industry. The whole of Hong Kong also depends on the mainland for its water and food supplies, and it must help control the border in order to prevent mass migration into the territory.

An agreement on the future of Hong Kong between the government of Great Britain and the government of the People's Republic of China states the situation.

The Chinese Government has consistently taken the view that the whole of Hong Kong is Chinese territory. Its position for many years was that the question of Hong Kong came under the category of unequal treaties left over from history; that it should be settled peacefully through negotiations when conditions were ripe; and that pending a settlement, the status quo should be maintained

The decolonization of Hong Kong has to be seen in relation to China's desire to reunify all its former territory. China has considered Hong Kong's return to China inevitable, and since the time of Mao, Beijing has considered Taiwan a top priority in the process of reunification. Since 1978, China has stopped calling for Taiwan's "liberation" and has instead looked toward "peaceful reunification of the motherland," with Taiwan having a degree of administrative autonomy. In fact, the "one country, two systems" policy was conceived of with Taiwan, rather than Hong Kong, in mind.

Steps Along the Way

In 1979 Sir Murray MacLehose became the first Hong Kong governor to pay an official visit to China. No one expected him to raise the issue of the lease, even though Hong Kong's commercial sector had become insistent on reaching a settlement. China was not prepared then to discuss land leases beyond 1997, but Deng told MacLehose, "Investors should set their hearts at ease." Confidence soared, and Hong Kong property became the most expensive in the world.

Two years later Deng proposed the "one country, two systems" formula to solve the dilemma of Hong Kong's future. The policy accomplished two things: it maintained the stability of Hong Kong and it advanced the goal of a unified China. To have socialism and capitalism existing side by side struck many as a creative solution to the problem "left over by history." In 1982 Deng said more explicitly that China would regain sovereignty over Hong Kong while preserving its market economy.

Residents of Hong Kong, Taiwan, and Macao felt encouraged when they studied China's new draft constitution, which provided a legal basis for the implementation of "one country, two systems" by empowering the state to establish "special administrative regions" and endow them with laws differing from those prevailing in the rest of the country. In 1982 the draft constitution was approved by the National People's Congress.

That same year British Prime Minister Margaret Thatcher visited Beijing and adamantly insisted that the British administer the territory beyond 1997. China refused to negotiate any British administrative presence in Hong Kong beyond 1997. Britain had to comply if it wished to maintain or expand an economic presence in China and southeast Asia.

Also in 1982 Hong Kong District Board held elections, unprecedented in the colony's history. The results revealed substantial political concerns over the colony's future particularly among young people.

The following year, China announced it would make no changes to Hong Kong for 50 years beyond 1997—a new experiment that would lead to eventual full integration with the mainland in 2047. While officials promised that the economic system would not change, they made no promises about the political situation. Any reference to British administration after 1997 had to be dropped. On 12 July 1983 formal negotiations began between China and Britain on the future of Hong Kong, Britain eventually dropping its request to continue administering the territory.

In January 1984 a demonstration denouncing the legitimacy of British rule turned violent; there were no deaths, but 30 people were injured—the worst riots in the territory since 1967. The demonstrations revealed that the Hong Kong government was weak and transient. Public confidence deteriorated further when Deng announced that People's Liberation Army troops would be stationed in Hong Kong after 1997. In the fall, Britain and China initialed the Joint Declaration on the Question of Hong Kong (see Appendix). The

Hong Kong's 1997 flag with a white bauhinia flower on a red ground symbolizing the "one country, two systems" policy

National People's Congress of China endorsed the agreement into law.

The agreement calls for Hong Kong people to rule Hong Kong as a Special Administrative Region—the HKSAR—from 1997 to 2047, after which the territory will become fully integrated with the mainland. Hong Kong will fly the Chinese flag, as well as the HKSAR flag, which carries a bauhinia flower. The socialist system and social policies practiced in the rest of the People's Republic will not be extended to the HKSAR. Hong Kong has been promised a high degree of autonomy, except in matters of foreign affairs and defense; units of the Chinese Army and Chinese naval vessels will be stationed in Hong Kong.

Clearly this was a negotiated resolution rather than an aggressive takeover. Hong Kong's return will be a major step toward a unified China. Access to international markets will add luster to China's "Four Modernizations" program and open-door economic policy. Britain, in maintaining a favorable relationship with China, will "retreat with honor," without taking several million Hong Kong emigrants along with it.

Many believe that Hong Kong people were denied a role during the Sino-British talks and resent their lack of opportunity to deliberate their own future. Margaret Thatcher used an analogy of a "three-legged stool" in an attempt to allow the three parties—the Chinese government, the British Parliament, and the citizens of Hong Kong—to be involved in the negotiations. China, however, has consistently held to the belief that the issue is a matter for only the two sovereign powers. Having no input in this "external matter," Hong Kong citizens were represented in an "internal matter"—the drafting of the Basic Law (see Appendix), Hong Kong's "mini-constitution" after 1997. The law was promulgated by the Chinese Congress in 1990. The Tiananmen Square tragedy of June 1989 caused the Hong Kong government to examine the need for a more representative system than the indirectly elected Legislative Council. By the 1990s, demands for democracy were too strong to ignore.

The appointment in 1992 of Christopher Patten as Hong Kong's 28th, and presumably last, governor signaled a new phase in this debate. Where the Basic Law did not specify otherwise, he sought to enlarge the franchise of voters during the 1995 elections. In a sampling of public opinion, 80 percent of Hong Kong residents approved.

Sino-British negotiations on Hong Kong's political reform proposals broke down again and again. By early 1994, it became clear that whatever reforms were instituted before 1997 would be scrapped after the Chinese took control of Hong Kong; indeed the National People's Congress Standing Committee in Beijing voted in August 1994 to terminate Hong Kong's political structure on 1 July 1997. China has stressed again and again the need to return to an executive-led system that would place more trust in civil servants than in a legislative council. The new HKSAR chief executive will be chosen by a committee controlled by Beijing and by Hong Kong's political and economic elite. In fact, Beijing has underscored the need for the civil service to be the most stabilizing force during the time of transition. It has also appointed four sets of advisers to China on Hong Kong affairs, who must have proven their loyalty to Beijing—or be rich and influential.

If businesses stay beyond 1997, Hong Kong will perhaps become the premier Asian city of the 21st century. If they leave, it will fade into a shadow of its former self. It won't be enough that its geographic location makes it ideal for regional corporate headquarters or that it will remain a window between China and the rest of the world. High rents, restrictions on freedoms, and the possible deterioration of law and order could make it prohibitive to conduct business in Hong Kong. Some companies are already selling off their properties and renting the space back until they see what happens. Empty, boarded-up buildings plastered with the telephone numbers of real estate agents cause business people to tremble.

It says something of Hong Kong's durability that it has always functioned well, acting quickly to provide for community needs and prospering even during times of global recession. It has earned a place in the *Guinness Book of World Records* for the generosity of its charitable donations. Like a village, it is a community that shares and cares—a characteristic that may become more important as the time of transition nears.

Half of the population of Hong Kong fled, or were born into families that fled, China during less stable times. What, then, does "love of China" mean for Hong Kong people? "If it means a sense of belonging to China as a civilization, everyone would be in favor," said Dr. Peter Lee. If it means the acceptance of the PRC as the sovereign authority, obviously, those who remain in Hong Kong would agree. But if "love of China" means the unquestionable devotion to the present regime of the PRC without any right to offer opinions for change in the structure and style of government, then it would be a different matter. Hong Kong's status as a Special Administrative Region permits multiple political parties. China, by contrast, does not tolerate any party opposing the Communist Party.

Some in China see Hong Kong as home to a lazy, rich, unpatriotic people—a place of subversion that needs to be punished. From the perspective of Hong Kong, China sometimes appears crime-ridden and inefficient, ruled by an indecisive government torn by power struggles. Their relationship—with all of its attendant misunderstandings, stereotypes, and suspicions—is extremely delicate. But the vigorous inflow of foreign capital and modern business practices make Hong Kong more indispensable than ever to China. Given these economic realities, Hong Kong and China have no other choice but to make this crucial transition together.

Implications of Reunification for the Economy and Society

As it changed from an opium emporium to one of the great trade ports of the world, Hong Kong long ago established its free market credentials—summed up best, perhaps, by Sir Philip Haddon-Cave, a long-time Hong Kong financial secretary, who said, "Let people and business do what they will." Over the years, the free market has operated with minimum interference, and industry has paid lower wages than it would have otherwise, because the government's vast public housing program has provided cheap subsidized housing for workers. Law and order, "liberty and the rule of law," minimum interference in private affairs, and the absence of import tariffs or controls on the movement of capital have long been the hallmarks of the Hong Kong way of doing business and running the territory. However, it shouldn't be forgotten that this environment, so conducive to profitable free enterprise, has allowed little participation in government and has had no minimum-wage legislation, no equal-opportunity legislation, and an ideologically split trade-union movement.

The big question at stake is how a unique economic and social entity will look when faced with the reality of "one country, two systems"—especially since the ideological cornerstone of the People's Republic has been to empower workers and the poor. Will the local representative of the Communist Party outrank the new HKSAR chief executive?

The notion of "one country, two systems" is not as impossible as one might imagine, according to Peter Lee. There has been an astonishing influx of capital from China to participate in the Hong Kong capitalist system. At the same time, parts of mainland China have opened to investments from Hong Kong in various forms of partnership with business interests in China, and China has been moving toward a market economy as exemplified by Hong Kong.

Politically Hong Kong will retain a high degree of "self government" under the "guidance" of the Communist Party. Noninterference and mutual respect are implied, but whether these principles will be honored remains to be seen.

Concern for Security

One of the most immediate problems facing Hong Kong is physical security. The job of keeping order in Hong Kong has been up to the colony's police force; currently 1 police officer serves every 174 people.

Hong Kong has enjoyed one of the lowest crime rates in the world. China has voiced its support for maintaining continued law and order in Hong Kong by keeping the civil service intact. While this is reassuring, it has also caused some jitters—not to mention some resignations and early retirements—for members of the police force, who will be asked to keep Hong Kong calm during the time of transition. Surveys indicate that nearly 6 in 10 civil servants plan to stay in Hong Kong.

One security concern yet to be worked out are extradition arrangements. During the 1990s, 95 countries held extradition agreements with Hong Kong. If citizens charged with crimes in their home countries arrived in Hong Kong with valid visas, they could be sent back to be tried. When Hong Kong reverts to Chinese rule, these arrangements cease, making the territory vulnerable to foreign criminals seeking refuge from justice. This situation is of particular concern because Hong Kong, as well as China, had been listed by the White House as a major hub of the drug traffic, although a 1995 U.S. State Department report commended Hong Kong for its superb efforts to curb the smuggling of narcotics.

Another security concern is illegal immigration, mostly of desperate, unemployed people arriving from the mainland. Many are "helped" to enter the colony by Hong Kong crime rings and the infamous triads (highly organized criminal gangs that originated in China, similar to the Mafia) in exchange for large sums of money. If they cannot pay their passage, they are often forced into slave labor and prostitution.

All illegal immigrants to Hong Kong are repatriated upon arrest. Employers who knowingly employ illegal immigrants are liable for a maximum fine of HK $250,000 (U.S. $32,500) and up to three years imprisonment. In 1993 some 35,193 illegals from China were arrested, a 4.4 percent increase over 1992. Illegal immigration alarms many residents; those living in public housing estates and squatter settlements feel uneasy on account of the increase in crime posed by the new arrivals. "My parents don't want me to attend church fellowship on a Saturday night anymore because it is not safe returning to my home," said Chan Wai-Ling, a church member.

Jobs and Labor Problems

Barges and ships headed for the South China Sea still move through the early morning mists in the harbor. Arms and legs glide in unison as old and young practice *taiji quan* (*tai chi*) in parks and open spaces. Scaffolding still adorns buildings under construction. The young people from crowded public housing estates still breeze through glitzy malls with no money to spend. And Hong Kong still works and reaches out to maintain its prosperity.

These conditions notwithstanding, the city designed for money making is finding itself squeezed out of breath. Pollution is increasing. Investors want an economy with high rates of growth and low levels of taxes. Hard-working people are unprotected, while businesses are allowed to compete unchecked. A stable government and an ideology sympathetic to business remain of paramount importance, yet, there are no guarantees of these.

With China's economic opening up in the early1980s, many factories moved from Hong Kong to China to avoid the high cost of labor and rent in Hong Kong's postwar economic boom and to take advantage of lower labor costs, unoccupied land, and fewer pollution controls. Moving provided a way to dodge union activities in Hong Kong and strikes for higher wages and better working conditions. (China has no independent unions to speak of.) The consequent displacement of workers disrupted many families. The territory, famous for its ubiquitous "Made in Hong Kong" label, was depleted of production-line jobs. In their place arose new jobs—in finance, industry, and hotel service—which required retraining for workers, as few spoke English.

Hong Kong exacerbated the economic dislocation of the early 1980s by importing cheap labor from the mainland and other parts of Asia. A Hong Kong construction worker may ask HK $950 (US $130) a day, whereas a worker from China accepts HK $350 (US $45). Imported workers are not only cheaper, they also take undesirable jobs that better-trained Hong Kong residents refuse, and they accept short-term contracts. Many restaurants, for example, change their work force every two years, avoiding the need for them to pay the severance and benefits the law requires for permanent employees. These workers prop up the local economy and also help the economy of their home country by sending remittances back to their families. Theirs is not an easy life. Some are abused, others find they have to work at two jobs to make ends meet.

Industry Problems

From the 1950s on, manufacturing combined the territory's good supply of labor, entrepreneurship, skill, and capital—much of it newly arrived from Shanghai—with advanced technology from Britain, the United States, and Japan. But in joining the hyper-growth of the postwar period, many companies compromised their standards. They flooded Western markets with gadgets, plastic flowers, toys, and fleeting clothes fashions. When other countries began to produce such items at lower cost, Hong Kong had to specialize its production and turn more to providing services.

Land reclamation projects involving the relocation of boat people

As textiles and other industries moved to China and elsewhere in Asia in search of cheaper labor, there were more and more displaced workers, especially older people with less education. In 1993 the Hong Kong government began a retraining program to help such workers. Employers still prefer younger, better-educated people for service-sector jobs. Many older women who have been left jobless cry, "We want manufacturing back." That refrain is also heard in the families of migrant husbands and fathers who work as technical staff or managers of the relocated textile factories. Some of them establish second families in the new work place. According to a 1995 estimate, some 240,000 Hong Kong children have fathers who now work in China. Their absence has caused enormous hardship as mothers try to keep families together and disenchanted young people become alienated from family life and make the streets their home.

Hong Kong's second largest industry is tourism. The territory ranks as the sixth most popular tourist destination in the world and television announcements implore residents to be nice to tourists. However, tourism experienced a serious slump after the 1989 Tiananmen Square tragedy; moreover, there are now fewer tourists from Japan and more from China. As a result, many retail stores that catered to the Japanese (wealthier than most Chinese) have closed. Finally, with the general strengthening of the Hong Kong economy, things simply aren't as cheap as they used to be. Shoppers discover that bargains are few and far between.

The "eating industry" has long been a major employer in Hong Kong. The city has thrived on being a restaurant culture—indeed, it is one of the great culinary capitals of the world. Business and social life revolve around Chinese restaurants and small eating shops (*dai pai dongs*). With economic uncertainty and creeping unemployment, eating habits have changed a bit: More people are eating and entertaining at home. Others are beating a track to an instant cup of noodles from 24-hour establishments. Many of the 6,000-odd licensed restaurants are shutting down as soaring rents and labor costs price them out of business. Only the top hotel restaurants can afford the best Chinese chefs, who have attained mastery after years of exacting, humble apprenticeship. Teamwork under pressure to clean kitchens and prepare vegetables is increasingly done by mainland women aged 25 to 40 who are willing to accept rock-bottom wages on two-year contracts. Employers prefer imported workers, who will work late nights and weekends, to locals, who want regular hours.

Problems also beset the fishing industry. As land-reclamation projects rush ahead on the Hong Kong and Kowloon shorelines, newspaper headlines scream, "Don't shrink our harbor to a river." With the narrowing of the harbor that separates the two shorelines, the waters around Hong Kong have become rougher. Increased water traffic has led to more accidents. The combination of increased water traffic, increased water pollution from land developments (such as the new Chek Lap Kok Airport), more work available on shore, and relocation inland by the government to avoid typhoons has made it unattractive or impossible to live on junks and sampans. Still another threat are mainland fishermen who use illegal fishing methods and mainland pirates. In the 1980s the number of Tanka (boat people) dwindled to less than 1 percent of the population. In the 1990s it was far less. Their way of life probably won't survive; few Hong Kong young people—even those who were ferried ashore by their grandparents, bound for school in crisp British-style school uniforms—want to rear their families in the old way. In the meantime, fisher folk are being replaced by mainland fishermen willing to undertake hazardous deep fishing trips.

The Need for Housing

Nothing in Hong Kong is as dramatic as the sheer density of people on so little land. Only 34 square miles out of a total of 412 square miles is residential. New immigrants have built squatter settlements on mountainsides, but these are being cleared for expensive housing and office developments close to the new airport. The residents of these settlements face despair—not only are their homes taken from them, but they cannot

76

afford even the subsidized public housing. Worse, they would have a long wait for such housing even if they could it afford it—there are already 172,000 people on the waiting list.

The history of public housing in Hong Kong began in 1953, when 53,000 people were left homeless on Christmas Day by a fire in the Shek Kip Mei squatter area. Out of that disaster was born the Hong Kong Housing Authority, which now provides rental and self-owned flats of increasingly higher standard for about 3 million people, half of the territory's population. Even with these high numbers, however, prices are too high and there are not enough apartments.

Hing Wah housing project for contract workers

In times of mass influx of refugees from China, miracles of hillside engineering were undertaken to house workers close to industrial areas. All that could be provided for them was a few feet of bunk space, windows with a pole for hanging laundry, and a small space for cooking. When workers were persuaded to move to the New Territories, agricultural land there was taken for housing. Today, housing projects are everywhere in the New Territories, producing an unusual, and sometimes uneasy, effect in an area of rural serenity. A Hong Kong Christian Service social worker who tries to help the families of contract laborers in temporary housing near the new airport says, "I came back to work here because the people have so much hope for just a small improvement. It is such a contrast to people who have so much that they no longer appreciate the small but important things in life."

An Education, but in What Language?

The two official languages of Hong Kong are Cantonese, the Chinese dialect spoken in Hong Kong and nearby Guangdong Province, and

English. However, Hong Kong is quickly becoming a trilingual city. With the approach of 1997, the need to learn Mandarin, or *putonghua* (the common language), is becoming more pressing. Some are dismayed, believing that Mandarin represents another unwelcome incursion by Beijing into the life of Hong Kong.

There is another, practical way to look at the issue. Employment depends largely on language competence. Bridging the gaps between the local majority (who speak Cantonese), the mainland, and the international world of trade (whose language is English) is becoming the norm. Classified ads stipulate "good written and spoken English and Chinese essential." It is no longer a given that "Chinese" means Cantonese; fluency in Mandarin has now become essential in many quarters. (A "fourth" language is also needed, the language of computers.)

There is also concern about people's true competence in English. Even though 90 percent of secondary-school education is officially in English, teaching has developed in "mixed code." Students using English textbooks and writing exams in English are instructed in Cantonese. Often secondary-school graduates have to be retrained for English-language courses at university; meanwhile, some worry that English may be thrown out as a colonial remnant rather than retained as an international necessity. Parents in Hong Kong, whether or not they are competent in English, consider English essential for their children as a passport for securing a good local job or for going abroad to study or work. Unfortunately Hong Kong lacks qualified English teachers because many of them have joined the business community or gone abroad.

Whatever the language, the intense, high-pressure rush of life in Hong Kong is mirrored in the classroom. With 40 or more students per teacher, there is little time for individual attention. Teachers say they lack the training to deal with the complications of their students' lives. Within a year, four teachers committed suicide, and 120 students attempted to take their own lives.

Women's Place

Women suffer a disadvantage in Hong Kong's economy. "Women are the first to be displaced. It's not easy for a factory worker with limited education to be employed in a hotel or other service-sector job," says Alice Yuk, general secretary of the Hong Kong YWCA.

It requires a new style, working as a team member, not as an individual in a production line. Skills have to be learned in receiving instructions in a way, interacting and dressing appropriately—and after training, support is crucial. Empowerment is so much needed for greater participation, but in the church there is little place to meet. It's easier in a YWCA venue. It took some time for this group of community workers to begin to express their feelings and concerns and contribute to problem-solving in a constructive way. That is part of the training the YWCA provides.

This training was evident as a group of women community leaders—meeting as part of a monthly young women's leadership and career-training program—fervently discussed the Comprehensive Equal Opportunities Bill, which had been voted down in July 1995 by the Legislative Council. Proposed by Anna Wu, it would have gone beyond discrimination on the basis of sex and disability to include age, race, family and sexual orientation, religious and political convictions, union activities, and past criminal convictions. "We were disappointed it was voted down, though it's a welcome start that the more limited Sex Discrimination Bill and Disability Discrimination Bill did pass," Wu said. A commission for implementation will be set up in the future. The more comprehensive bill was voted down because of its potential to create disputes, require legal proceedings, and upset social harmony, said the Rev. Kwok Nai-Wang, director of the Hong Kong Christian Institute.

Especially subject to discrimination are women newly arrived from China, Alice Yuk said.

Another of our programs is in improving the quality of life . . . of new immigrants from China. This includes an "at home" program of cooking classes along with other services. When more women come from China requiring help with their educational background we could discuss with the government department concerned how best to help them overcome their difficulties.

Speaking about the Fourth UN Conference on Women in Beijing in September 1995, Yuk warned,

Care had to be taken that such a meeting brought women together rather than splitting them apart. The success of the conference will depend on what is done afterwards. The women's movement is a lifelong effort—it won't be achieved in one conference. To be united and strong in our movement we work with a coalition of other women's groups in Hong Kong. After 1997 we expect our work to continue much the same.

Leung Lai-Lin, a pastoral worker in Hong Kong, has a unique story to tell, although it begins like that of many other fellow residents.

My family came from Guangdong Province after 1949. From when I was born in Wan Chai, my father repaired shoes in a small space between a stall and a store. Unfortunately it got to a point where he didn't bring any money home because he gambled a lot. My mother was forced to go to work in a factory to support our family of four children, two girls and two boys. I was the second born. My elder brother went to secondary school all day. It was common for a male in grass-roots families to go to school as no matter how difficult the family situation, boys were expected to have a chance.

When I was 12 my grandmother objected to any further education for me. She had never been to school. My mother had [gone] for only a couple of years. They ended up quarreling about payment for my grandmother looking after us. Worried at hearing this, I volunteered to quit school to look after my younger brother and sister for a year. I don't think education to Form 3 [grade 9] was compulsory then, but I do remember some sadness because my academic achievement was good enough for me to do three years of secondary school.

When I was 13 in 1974, I worked in a small factory on the ground floor of the public housing estate where we lived. It was hard work on imitation ceramics for long hours. The HK $7 (U.S. $1) per day I earned went to my mother. When I was 14 I was of legal age to join her in a bigger factory. I worked in a plastics factory and then moved to electronics. Except for some textile worker jobs, chances of better pay for length of experience were remote. We changed every few years from boredom, if the system was not good, or if there were personnel problems.

When I was 19 years old my co-worker in the factory invited me to the Lutheran Church. That first time in church I was impressed to discover there is a God who really values people. Later I found a brochure at the church advertising English and labor law classes offered through the Blue Collar Evangelism Program at the Hing Wah Methodist Chapel. It was sponsored by a church in the United States [the United Methodist Church Advance Special]. The program was started by Mr. Leung Ying-On. He taught adult education, talked about China, and preached. Through this he enabled me to see more deeply that God really values persons, that irrespective of background, all are equal before God. I came to realize that we workers were the exploited, oppressed group and that spreading the gospel could help a person become a real human being. It was very important to me to learn to amalgamate service and the gospel.

I appreciated the preaching and belief in daily life of Rev. Lo Lung-Kwong, who was in charge of Epworth Village and started the Hing Wah Chapel. Besides he helped me have the vision to spread the gospel to blue-collar workers—it was an opportunity that changed my life. I found the members of Hing Wah to be very very keen in providing services and [I] later joined as a voluntary worker, identifying myself with spreading the gospel to blue-collar workers.

. . . One day I brought an acquaintance at the factory, Ms. Cheung Siu-Ling, to chapel. She is a part-time worker. At first she was very quiet, never speaking out. Her participation in Bible study and worship certainly changed that. She had a lot more confidence and we encouraged her to apply to be a clerical officer of the blue-collar project at the

Leung Lai-Lin, pastoral worker at Hing Wah Chapel, and one of the children in her care

chapel, which she did, continuing part-time when her children were small. Her husband is also a member and the whole family worships on a Saturday. Now we are colleagues at Hing Wah Methodist Chapel, Chai Wan, where I have been since July 1993. I live in parish worker quarters at Epworth Village.

The people to whom I minister all live nearby in a public housing estate of about 14,000 people outside factories. We used to take the "happy cart" with all kinds of activities to involve people. We played the guitar and sang—with a permit, of course. That drew many people. But few work in factories now as they've been moved to China. Besides the many elderly people there are career people, mainly women.

The majority work in service jobs such as in hotels, in sales, reception, and as messengers. They are hawkers, restaurant workers, truck drivers, plumbers, electricians, or contract laborers for construction projects. About 2,000 are Christians. My big concern is how to serve the different members of the families who work long hours, often until 11 P.M. I learned from the beginning that many could not come to worship because Sunday was not their day off, so additional worship services were started on Saturday evenings and afternoons for the elderly so more could attend. In Tsim Sha Tsui in Kowloon many people in the "eating industry" meet for fellowship on Fridays when they come off duty from restaurants at 11:45 P.M.

Economic pressures in Hong Kong have become very great. Each week I am in touch with three groups of people: women, singles, and the elderly. Women face hardships as they can't work when their babies are young, yet they need to spend more because of their children. The majority only have education below Form 3 so need help in finding a new job when factories move to China. It's hard to find a job if you're a displaced factory worker over 30. We provide child care . . . so that homemakers can attend the activities provided for women on alternative Fridays. It started with cooking lessons and developed into many interest groups and seminars. They learn about looking after and teaching children. They also develop skills in handicrafts for fun, recreation, and income. This way I get in touch with the whole family and it makes a difference because it is particularly difficult to spread the gospel to males of the grass-roots class.

In grass-roots work you must be prepared to give more than you get back. Lots of time goes into establishing relationships. A relationship you tried hard to establish can end abruptly when a young woman gets a boyfriend and moves away. The singles are keen to learn how better to relate to people. Repetitive work in factory production lines has not developed skills at relating.

About two years ago, I found many women coming from China on two-year contracts to work in restaurants. They live in housing in Chai Wan provided by their employers. I think about it a lot but we haven't yet developed programs to reach out to them.

Hong Kong is more than a vast housing estate providing cheap labor for the service industries—labor seethes with unfulfilled expectations.

Youth: Problems and Promise

As in the rest of the world, the cultural heritage of Hong Kong youth is quickly becoming linked to the three M's: Marlboro, McDonald's, and MTV. Hong Kong offers its young people parks, sports and recreational facilities, youth centers, playgrounds, youth hostels, summer camps, and access to the outlying islands. But this is a tough, competitive city, and its society is very commercialized. For many of those who will not go on for higher education and feel "stuck," life becomes a search for identity and companionship that is fulfilled only by taking drugs or joining gangs and triad societies.

An average of 42 young people are arrested each day, with offenses ranging from serious assaults, drug possession, and burglary to triad-related offenses such as extortion or gang fighting. In 1994 a crime committed by a child under 10 took place every 12 days. Offenses against property have greatly increased in the last 20 years.

A YMCA survey indicated that rather than attending activities organized by social-service agencies such as youth centers, many young people prefer to hang around snack shops, gambling stalls, billiard rooms, all-night pubs, discos, bowling centers, and karaoke lounges. These are not necessarily the best places to meet worthwhile friends: of the 61 percent who say they meet new friends in game centers, nearly a third have been asked to join the triad societies.

This, of course, is not a complete picture. Not all young people are congregating in at-risk locales. Still, highly commercialized as it is, Hong Kong is not an easy place in which to grow up. Particularly among younger people, religious faith tends to be overshadowed by the forces of materialism, secularism, and scientific and technological progress. Many feel they do not have the time to pay attention to spiritual matters. Nevertheless, if given the chance to discover the spiritual dimension of life, they may be inspired to search for solid values and religious convictions.

The Plight of the Elderly

Hong Kong, like other developed countries, has an aging population. While other Asian countries have relatively younger populations, the percentage of the elderly in Hong Kong is second only to that of Japan, which has a higher percentage of aging than any other country in the world. Whereas Hong Kong's population increases by about 3 percent at five-year intervals, those over 65 are expected to increase by more than 10 percent by the year 2006. As 85 percent came from China, many elderly continue to suffer from low socioeconomic status and live in public housing estates. More than 8 out of 10 have primary education or less. As some younger family members have emigrated, numerous elderly have been left behind, often by their own free will, in order to stay with what they are used to.

The Family in Transition

Because the family is at the center of Chinese culture, changes in Hong Kong's circumstances that affect the family also affect society. During the years of British rule, most Hong Kong Chinese have lived according to a utilitarian family system, inherited from China. Generally the family looks after all members and often provides capital for new economic ventures. In return, an individual's behavior is directed toward providing for the economic security and social standing of the family. Family members place family interests above those of society or any class or party. For most, immediate material satisfaction is the priority, a point of view that makes for short-distance horizons.

There are signs, however, that the utilitarian family system is diminishing in importance. The large population of young people born in Hong Kong have not experienced the turmoil their parents went through. And through Westernized education, they have developed wider aspirations both for themselves and their society as a whole. They see themselves as being far less reliant on family then their elders were. This erosion of parental authority and diminishing of social control, occurring amidst Hong Kong's continual modernization, can make society much less stable.

The family focus has been a long-term guarantee of Hong Kong's political stability, but it has also made for very little participation in politics. Continuing the traditional Chinese attitude of bureaucratic paternalism and passive public acceptance of government, most people have enjoyed the efficient government and improved living conditions in Hong Kong. Thus issues that might have stirred discontent in other societies are diffused.

The fact that only a third of Hong Kong residents cast ballots in the 1995 Legislative Commission elections is proof that old patterns die hard. Blame it on the realities of colonialism, a refugee mentality, anxiety about Beijing, past discouragement of political activity, or the failure of the educational system—the fact is, Hong Kong is not a city of high political participation.

The attention focused on the economic realm, and the centrality of the family in economics contribute to Hong Kong's lack of true civic culture. Although a growing class of educated, politically aware people, particularly the young, have been calling for reform since the late 1960s, they have had to overcome much in their way. The colonial educational system, for example, has generally downplayed Hong Kong history and has generally taught Chinese history only up to 1911. Moreover, the governing ethos of the city, and thus the education system as a whole, focused on economic upward mobility and downplayed the need to cultivate critical political thinking or a sense of citizenship.

With Beijing's dismissal of the recent Hong Kong efforts at political reform, the future of this politicized class is unclear. Many who see involvement in politics as a way to improve society see emigration as the only solution.

Implications of Reunification for the Church

Before 1949, church growth in Hong Kong was slow, with only a few congregations being established by mainline denominations. Travel between Hong Kong and the mainland was frequent, particularly during the years of Japanese occupation. Close ties existed between the churches in Hong Kong and those across the border. Foreign missionary societies provided social and educational services and were instrumental in training many of the colony's community and government leaders. The churches in Hong Kong today have moved from dependence on foreign mission boards to independence. This change is rooted in the late 1960s, when overseas church mission boards and agencies made plans for gradual withdrawal from Hong Kong. Hong Kong churches, more indigenized and anxious for autonomy, began to generate their own income. Many of the church schools and hospitals are now funded with government assistance. In turn, well over half of Hong Kong's social-service agencies and more than 40 percent of its schools are run by the churches.

Hong Kong churches are trying to be more responsive to the needs of the poor and marginalized, but they are also having to meet the needs of a whole range of society that is about to undergo a major transition. Fear, prejudice, anger, and other obstacles to the transition have to be addressed by clergy and laity, who themselves are caught up in the same emotions. Although the Basic Law declared by China has guaranteed the right of worship, Hong Kong churches will have to discover what that right means in the new era.

China's Reaffirmation of the Role of Hong Kong Churches

At the invitation of the China State Council's Bureau of Religious Affairs, a delegation of 19 representatives of major Protestant denominations, seminaries, and evangelical organizations in Hong Kong visited Beijing in November 1991. The delegation presented a situation paper of "opinions" and suggestions concerning the church and the social situation of the 1997 transition.

Happily, Chen Zhiying, deputy director of the China State Council's Hong Kong and Macao Affairs office, made clear that the HKSAR government would not interfere in the internal affairs of religious organizations or control any religious activities that do not violate the laws of the HKSAR. They would enjoy all legal rights, religious freedom, and opportunities for social service guaranteed by the Basic Law.

Neither the Religious Affairs Bureau nor the church in China would interfere in the religious affairs of Hong Kong. A religious organization, according to the Basic Law, will have the right to possess, use, manage, inherit, give, and receive property. Religious organizations will be able to continue to establish schools, seminaries, hospitals, social-welfare agencies, and other social services, according to existing policies. They will be able to maintain and develop relationships with religious organizations in other parts of the world, and their relations to religious organizations in China should be according to the principles of nonsubordination, noninterference, and mutual respect.

The Hong Kong delegation also met with Bishop K. H. Ting, president of the China Christian Council, who emphasized that churches in China and Hong Kong should have more exchanges.

These policies were embodied in the Basic Law. In 1994 a group of non-Chinese Christians in Hong Kong issued a statement, saying that the new sets of regulations are in some ways the codification of practices which have been in place for some time. Their promulgation represents a small step forward in the promotion of the rule of law in China.

We do not interpret these regulations as being "new restrictions on religious freedom" imposed by the government. While we might hope that someday all restrictions on religion would be lifted, we note that there are similar practices limiting the scope of foreign missionary activity in many Asian countries. Our work, which is done in partnership with Chinese churches, has not been affected at all by the new regulations, and we hope it will not be.

Social Service and the Hong Kong Christian Council

Since government services are inadequate and the family system of support is fading, there is more and more social work for the churches to do. According to Tso Man-King, general secretary of the HKCC, churches in Hong Kong are entrusted by the government with running more than 60 percent of the social-service agencies and more than 40 percent of its schools. They provide more than 20 percent of the hospital beds.

Some of this work is done by denominations through their own district ministries. The Anglican Diocese of Hong Kong and Macao has given special attention to lay leadership training and work with new immigrants from China. The Methodist Church, meanwhile, is redeveloping rundown properties rather than taking its money out of Hong Kong, as some in the church have suggested it do.

Family of new contract worker aided by Hong Kong Christian Service

Much social ministry is carried on by the church-related groups such as the YMCA and YWCA. They support youth programs, youth camps and retreats, and arts and music programs. The YMCA offers vocational training and other job-related services. Caritas, the umbrella of social services in the Catholic Church, has a similar program. Christian Action

MINISTRY TO VIETNAMESE BOAT PEOPLE

The 1975 Communist victory in Vietnam caused thousands of civilians—many of whom had helped the American military and diplomatic services—to flee the country. Also fleeing were those who feared death and "reeducation," because of their middle-class status or the role they played with the South Vietnamese government. Others fled because of their fear of persecution for their religious beliefs. In 1978 some 2,000 refugees a month poured out of the country because of Vietnam's decision to nationalize private businesses and resettle city dwellers on agricultural communes.

They fled overland through jungles to Thailand, or by boats across treacherous seas to Malaysia, the Philippines, Hong Kong, Singapore, and Thailand. Facing shipwreck, pirates, starvation, murder, rape, and robbery, 60 percent died.

Of those who survived, many landed in Hong Kong on their way to other countries. They felt frustrated and desperate, particularly when the United States—the place many wanted to go—endorsed a repatriation policy by the Hong Kong government, whereby immigrants would be returned to Vietnam.

In 1979 Hong Kong offered temporary asylum, allowing refugees to stay until resettlement. The Hong Kong Christian Service ran a camp for 10,000 Vietnamese refugees between 1978 and 1981. Christian groups maintained open access to centers for ministries and services. The focus of such activity was the Kaitak Center, which was taken over from the Red Cross in 1987 by the Hong Kong Christian Aid to Refugees (now called Christian Action). The programs in refugee camps and detention centers are vital to prepare the refugees for integration in resettlement countries or reintegration on return to Vietnam. Services have included vocational training, dental health services, recreation for children, and programs for pregnant women.

The refugees have long faced a poor public image in overcrowded, insecure Hong Kong. "A tiny minority may be termed bad elements," said one Christian worker in the camps, "but the majority are fine, hard-working, gifted people."

Beijing has made it clear that it will not recognize Hong Kong as a first place of asylum for Vietnamese migrants after 1997. All camps will be cleared.

cooperates with the government's program to retrain workers, providing training, job orientation, placement, and follow-up counseling.

A great deal of social-service work is done through the Hong Kong Christian Council, especially in the Hong Kong Christian Service, an arm of the HKCC with more than 500 full-time and 200 part-time staff members. The staff works toward building a caring community and working with the greater Hong Kong community in forming public policies and monitoring their implementation. Services are provided that are effective for all sectors of the community, from the middle class to those who are most neglected, such as immigrant contract workers and the Vietnamese boat people.

Another function of the HKCC is to relate to a number of small, vital groups concerned with social justice and human-rights concerns. These include the Hong Kong Christian Industrial Committee, the Hong Kong Women's Christian Council (discussed in the section "Women in the Church"), and the Hong Kong Christian Institute.

The Christian Industrial Committee (CIC) tries to aid workers. It helped draft labor laws that called for accident compensation, severance pay, and maternity leave. Through contact with the committee, its present director, Lau Chin-Shek, an immigrant who was elected to the Hong Kong Legislative Council in 1991, became a Christian. He worked for paid maternity leave for women, the settlement of labor disputes, and labor education. Because of his efforts and those of others on the committee, evangelistic outreach to workers became a priority. For example, it was difficult for Christian workers to be accepted by middle-class congregations, so a church for workers was established in Kwun Tong.

Women in the Church

Sixty percent of Hong Kong Chinese Christians are women, points out Lily Lau of the HKCC's Women's Committee, which was formed in 1975. "These 300,000 women share the same problems as other women in society: traditional and cultural stereotyping. This is a big loss both to women and the church as lack of theological reflection limits members' growth." The council is dedicated to going beyond "remedial" action. Its new programs and projects include training in self-esteem and assertiveness, as well as addressing the issues of training women pastors and dealing with women's work in the church.

The council has organized fellowship groups for foreign household workers and offers them Bible study, worship services, and special programs of assistance. In conjunction with the YWCA it trains women volunteers and provides occupational training for mid-life homemakers.

At the heart of all programs is the need for further theological reflection on the role of women in church and society—of all women, whether they are professionals, marginalized, homemakers, or prostitutes. Central, too, is the fact that Jesus respected women. Can the church be a leader in emphasizing the value of the experience of women? The HKCC is trying to help the churches and the wider society answer these questions positively.

A WOMAN IN THE VANGUARD

"It can be an advantage when older people, who have stopped the whole world moving, leave Hong Kong," said the Rev. Lee Ching-Chee, associate general secretary of the Hong Kong Council of the Church of Christ in China. "Younger, less stubborn clergy are then forced to lead the church, and congregations seem to express themselves more freely in ways they hadn't dared before. With clergy and lay people tending to think more, there is more openness for education and inner struggle."

Lee is one of the first ordained Hong Kong clergywoman. Initially a school teacher, she was baptized in her early 20s and was nominated to be a Church of Christ in China (Hong Kong) executive while still quite young. She later received a scholarship to study in Great Britain. "Representing the HKCCC at the World Council of Churches . . . in Uppsala in 1968 changed my thinking," she said. "For a Hong Kong person from a conservative background, it was eye-opening. I became more ecumenical. What impressed me was that women's representation and the need for more youth participation was questioned and the program to combat racism, which greatly influenced changes in South Africa, were launched."

Lee, together with the Rev. Paul Ng, represent their denomination on the Theology Division Board of Chung Chi College. Lee also was formerly a trustee of the United Board for Christian Higher Education in Asia. "A problem is that some young people, having had no say all their lives, don't know how to say things even when given the opportunity," she said. "Ministers can help them use their brains instead of remaining humble and quiet. More people are getting hurt and more healing is needed—the church has charge of a healing ministry. When we as the church don't just sit expecting to enjoy ourselves but are with the people, there is hope."

Independent of the HKCC's Women's Council is the Hong Kong Women's Christian Council (HKWCC). Founded by 35 local women in 1988, it works for the empowerment of Christian women through education and action. Members of HKWCC and other supporters such as some

Catholic groups, seminaries, and local pastors, actively work for peace, justice, and "equality according to God's will both within churches and society." In the church, HKWCC has attempted to develop a feminist theology and a feminist resource center, promote new Christian women leaders, and support women marginalized by both church and society such as prostitutes, divorced women, factory workers, and migrant workers. It is concerned with separate taxation for spouses, the right of women to inherit land in the New Territories, shelters for abused women, and recently, lesbian issues.

Six percent of Hong Kong clergy are women (as compared to 14 percent in China). In 1993 there were 30 theologically trained and ordained women in the territory. They include five members of the Church of Christ in China, six Lutherans, six Methodists, five Anglicans, two from Pentecostal Holiness churches, two from Assemblies of God churches, and four from independent churches. One of the first ordinations of a woman, an Anglican, was in 1944, but progress was slow. One of the next women to be ordained was the Rev. Lee Ching-Chee of the Hong Kong Council of the Church of Christ in China, in 1966.

Theological Education

Hong Kong is home to 13 theological training centers. Among them are the Lutheran Seminary, Baptist Seminary, China Graduate School of Theology, and Alliance Seminary, all of which tend to attract students from evangelical and fundamentalist backgrounds. The Lutheran Seminary has been receiving students selected by the China Christian Council to do graduate work in Hong Kong. Perhaps most unique is the Theological Division of Chung Chi College because it is the only Protestant theological training unit within a Chinese university. Chung Chi's roots are in the union of Lutheran, Reformed, Methodist, United Church, and Anglican missions, and it carries the tradition of 13 Christian universities in China. While Chung Chi College itself is subsidized by the Hong Kong government, the Theological Division is responsible for its own funding. There are frequent exchanges between the division and the seminaries.

The Rev. Lo Lung-Kwong, the new head of the Theological Division, notes that during the last 50 years, the church in Hong Kong has been very active in social service and action. "An important issue in the history of the Chinese church and society has been how to contribute to society at large," he said. Those studying at Chung Chi—many of whom can't or don't want to study abroad—have the opportunity to ask these questions and develop theologically within a Chinese environment and in the context of a secular university.

A Chung Chi education is available not only for Hong Kong students but for those from the mainland as well. About half its graduates are pastors; the other half are teachers of theology and religious studies in church-related schools. Chung Chi is rooted in ecumenism and current theological progressivism: feminist theology is among the courses taught. It is also deeply committed to spiritual growth and fellowship.

Relations with the Church in China

The relationship between the churches in China and Hong Kong is often summed up by the phrase *qiu tong cun yi* (seeking the common ground while preserving the differences). Although Hong Kong churches fear possible government control after 1997, despite the assurances of the Basic Law, one of the Hong Kong Christian Council's priorities through the years has been forming ties with Christians on the mainland. The oldest effort between the two groups of churches began in 1974 with the Five Loaves and Two Fish campaign. This venture was the first overseas aid project initiated by the Hong Kong churches, and it has, over the years, channeled much relief aid to China as well as to other countries. Sponsored by the HKCC, the project is fully answerable to the church for administration and distribution. Another initiative, Project Nehemiah, helps rebuild churches in China's rural areas.

Rev. Lo Lung-Kwong, Rev. Lincoln Leung, Rev. Li Ping-Kwong, and Ms. Katherine Ng visiting a church in Guangzhou that Hong Kong churches helped renovate

Delegate of the China Christian Council meeting a Chinese Christian in Hong Kong

In 1979 a group of Hong Kong pastors led by the Rev. Lincoln Leung, president of the Methodist Church, Hong Kong, met with pastors in China. The same year the HKCC invited Chinese Christian leaders to visit Hong Kong Island to meet Hong Kong Christians. Since then, there have been numerous exchanges and visits. Ministers and theologians from Hong Kong have regularly been guest speakers in Chinese pulpits and seminaries, while theological students from Hong Kong have had exchanges with those in Nanjing Seminary and other theological centers. "We have so much to learn from each other and we have so much to share, including resources, which is much more than just remembering each other in prayers. The relationship will definitely be strengthened," said Tso Man-King, general secretary of the HKCC.

The encounters have proven essential because many Hong Kong Christians continue to have the wrong information about the church in China; some have never met Christians in China. In 1995 HKCC established a China Christian Liaison Committee, which enables Chinese churches to participate in joint-venture projects in Hong Kong. The aim is to promote an ecumenical spirit while avoiding projects that would promote denominationalism in the postdenominational church of China.

The HKCC explores potential projects with the China Christian Council, and refers them to churches in Hong Kong that are interested in providing long-term support. The idea is to avoid duplication of projects with other groups and agencies.

As just one example of this new-found cooperation between Hong Kong and Chinese Christians, the Methodist Church, Hong Kong, has developed ways to support and show concern for mainland churches. The interest took on a sense of immediacy in late 1993, when Hong Kong Methodists accepted an invitation from the Guangdong Christian Council and visited six towns in the Bei Jiang region, the area where the

British–related Methodist Church had concentrated its mission work prior to 1949. Among the results of this first trip were planning for a new church in the village of Shangtai. The visitors also saw the results of aid given to Hua Ying Primary School, named after a Methodist secondary school in Hong Kong. The Chinese school had been closed after 1949 but was recently reconstructed by the Hong Kong Christian Council's Five Loaves and Two Fish aid program. "The fact that the school is allowed to keep its former name is a treasure we shall keep in our hearts," said the Rev. Li Ping-Kwong, former president of the Methodist Church, Hong Kong. Now affiliated to the church in name only, the school is using its hall as a place for Sunday church services—a first for China, as even schools established by Chinese Christians are not permitted to function in a religious capacity.

Rebuilding program under the Five Loaves and Two Fish program

The churches in Hong Kong are still trying to determine how to strengthen their ties with the church in China now that 1997 ensures the two will have closer relations. "Theological education is one such concern, since mainland churches lack resources, particularly pastors and assistant pastors," said Li. "We are considering how we can help in this field."

In taking the long view of the years ahead, Wilson Chow of the Chinese Graduate School of Theology says, "We will be living and serving in China. Yet society will operate in a different system. There is the already and not-yet, continuity and discontinuity. That makes the differences and makes Hong Kong unique and strategic. We look eagerly forward to 1997 and beyond."

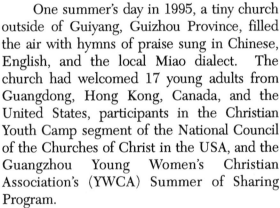

Chapter 4

Building Bridges
of Understanding

One summer's day in 1995, a tiny church outside of Guiyang, Guizhou Province, filled the air with hymns of praise sung in Chinese, English, and the local Miao dialect. The church had welcomed 17 young adults from Guangdong, Hong Kong, Canada, and the United States, participants in the Christian Youth Camp segment of the National Council of the Churches of Christ in the USA, and the Guangzhou Young Women's Christian Association's (YWCA) Summer of Sharing Program.

This country church was poor. It could not afford to offer its visitors fancy fruits or sugary pastries. But what it could provide for these strangers was friendship and hospitality in the name of Jesus the Christ. Over the entrance to the church, four characters exclaimed, "God loves the world's people" and inside, on its front wall surrounding the cross, "one faith, one Lord, one baptism."

Moved by the experience, one North American wrote, "Ordinary believers embraced us and sang with us and wept with joy with us. How important it is to experience the living faith that so many Christians in China have, and the aspirations that we share in the Spirit of God." Another participant from China, using her best English, said, "Before Summer of

Sharing I was afraid of foreigners. [Then] we saw each other's eyes when we were talking, that feeling was very warm!"

It is precisely this type of understanding that is helping to usher in a new era of missional relations with Christians throughout the world, especially within China. The church in China has asked for a reappraisal of past unequal relations and new, rather than renewed, relationships for the future. What does this mean? Together, how can we attempt to learn about and live God's mission in this ever changing world?

"Sending Churches"

Since the 19th century, churches in the West have understood themselves in terms of "sending" churches, implying rather arrogantly that only "we" have something to give to "them." This attitude also suggests there must be a "receiving" church that is unable to support or govern itself and is in need of funds, missionaries, and Western theology. These traditional patterns of mission fostered paternalism and dependency in the recipients. Some churches were created to fit precisely into these molds!

Coinciding with China's forced opening for economic gain by Western nations and Japan, China became the most important mission enterprise of the late 19th and early 20th centuries. Huge sums of money and personnel were poured into China to build schools and hospitals and churches. Indeed many missionaries did good work, but they also created the impression that the mission enterprise was performed by a mighty transnational religious corporation![1] Not until after 1949 were many of these church bodies willing to confront the theological and ethical dilemmas created by being part of the affluence of the "sending nation."[2]

Early missionaries were sometimes unaware of China's long-enduring history and civilization. "Sending" organizations expected these missionaries to carry to China not only the light of the Christian gospel but Western reason and inventiveness (ignoring that some "Western" inventions originated in China). Instead, missionaries discovered a proud people keenly aware of their own culture's unique accomplishments.

Neighbors in Mission

The church in China has been radically transformed since 1949. Chinese Christians claimed and found strength in their postdenominational independence. Exciting changes continue to take place, and the church in China is eager to share them with the world! Self-isolation is not one of the Three-Self principles.

North Americans can learn much from Christians in China: faithfulness amid significant sociopolitical change; how to be a servant people; the significant role of lay leadership, especially among women; the power of the grace of God found in forgiveness; the newness of the resurrection message as witnessed in the life of both the church and the nation; and the beauty of simplicity, even when a culture is 4,000 years old!

Early arrivals to be sure of a seat

In Luke 10: 25-37, Jesus tells the story of a traveler who was robbed, beaten, and left for dead. Along came a stranger, someone the traveler had been taught to hate and despise. The stranger, however, bandaged the man's wounds and even paid for a night's lodging.

How many times have we automatically put ourselves into the role of the Good Samaritan, assuming that only we can help them? The truth of the Christian community is that while today we may be the one offering bandages as another bleeds, tomorrow we may be the wounded, aching one who needs another's tender loving care. So it is in the world church and its global ministries. There is life-giving truth where there is mutuality in mission.

Christians in China recognize they have much to offer the rest of our world about God's revelation, and they wish to do so in partnership rather than in old patterns of mission paternalism. Explains Bishop K. H. Ting,

> We like to think of ourselves as an ellipse with two foci, which are not exclusive but mutually strengthening and enhancing—our particularity and our universality. All the good missionaries of the past have brought to China has not been lost, and we are grateful to them. Today, there are other ways for our church in China to benefit from churches abroad. A relationship of a new kind is not only possible but already emerging. Churches abroad can help us most by understanding our need to keep the two foci in good balance.[3]

The success of God's mission today depends on a healthy relationship. The responsibilities of giving and receiving must be shared by both partners. What are some of these responsibilities?

Papercut of the Good Samaritan

- respect for each other as equal members of the body of Christ (1 Cor. 12: 12-13)
- willingness to listen and understand, sometimes through honest struggle
- care and compassion, using Christ as a model
- putting God's love and passion for justice in a central place in our thinking

The China Christian Council's monthly magazine is entitled *Tianfeng*, meaning "Heavenly Wind." It is a beautiful description of the effect of the Holy Spirit in the lives of God's people throughout the world. This wind knows no boundaries. Neither is it confined to narrow nationalism or denominationalism. As this God-directed phenomenon touches us, how may we respond?

Empty Hands

One mission image may be that of empty hands:

Sometimes, especially for Western Christians, the "things" we bring with us in mission relationships get in our way. Our hands are so full of mission dollars, or teachers, or machinery, that we cannot reach out and touch the persons with whom we want to share. . . . However, all these gifts are from God and belong to God. They are not ours to give. And so we first need to place these gifts on God's altar. Then with our hands empty we can reach out and touch the people with whom we are in mission. By touching them and greeting them and getting to know them, we begin to develop a relationship based on who we are and not the "things" we offer.[4]

Attentive listening is the first step toward responsible action. In Luke 10: 36-42, Jesus commended Mary for first getting to know him, through listening to his teachings—much to the consternation of her sister, Martha, who thought she knew what Jesus needed (a decent meal) without even taking the time to ask!

How Christians in China Are in Mission

Christians in China see the church there as an instrument of renewal. Less than 1 percent of the total population, they don't see themselves in the majority any time soon. Their small number doesn't discourage them, however, from proclaiming the message of love and reconciliation so central to their understanding of the Christian gospel.

Following Christ's example, Christians in China combine faith and action to proclaim God's word. In a society where relationships are paramount, "Evangelism is seen as not only bringing Christ to men and women, but bringing Christ out of them so that people at both ends of the line of communication are receivers."[5]

In Gansu Province Christians in Yangwan are praised for their community spirit. They voluntarily organized a brigade from their congregation to widen the only road leading from their village. When the local government called for volunteers to plant trees on a barren mountainside to avoid further erosion of precious farm land, the response from the local villagers was discouraging. Yangwan Christians then organized a work team of 44 members, which accomplished the feat in no time.[6]

In rural Yunnan Province, the inhabitants of Baihua village, all of whom are Christian, were cited by the government as a model of moral character. Baihua is situated in an inaccessible mountain area, very close to the Golden Triangle, a region where the drug trade, violence, and prostitution are increasing. Baihua is extremely poor. While the incentive is great to grow illegal opium poppies, which would bring a high price, villagers have chosen to stick to producing food, which is not nearly so lucrative. A team of Beijing reporters who investigated the area were so moved by the spirit of a Sunday service, and by the exemplary simple life of the Lisu Christians, that they wrote a long article praising the Baihua inhabitants.[7]

Since 1983, Christians in Weifang in Shandong Province have operated the Three-Self Tea Company, whose profits augment the work of the church there. Income could be much higher if the shop sold cigarettes and alcoholic beverages along with tea, but church members refused to sell merchandise that they felt was harmful to the health of others. The shop is seen by Christians there as a means to make Christianity more visible within the city. All workers in the shop are Christian, and half-hour devotions are held every morning before business begins.[8]

Tianfeng is replete with stories of Christians in service to their communities. Bishop Ting helps explain why these acts resonate so deeply with the Chinese experience:

> In the country of Confucius, where the ethical approach is so deep-rooted and where to serve the good of the people becomes the common people's understanding of Marxism, to approach God ethically . . . is entirely natural and acceptable. People want to know how a Christian views goodness and where resources for a good life may be found. With the thought content of over ninety-nine percent of our people having nothing to do with Christianity, we welcome all positive views about Jesus. They are all fruits of evangelism, not quite so countable as heads of individual converts receiving baptism, but possibly more important in the long run.[9]

The Amity Foundation

One of the most effective ways through which Christianity is made more widely known to the Chinese people is the work of the Amity Foundation. Christian leaders initiated the Amity Foundation in 1985 as a way to be in social-service ministry among the Chinese people. Mindful of the colonial legacies of the past, Amity is an independent Chinese voluntary organization with outreach in health care, education, social welfare, rural development, relief and rehabilitation, and the printing of Bibles and Christian literature.

Amity's goals are threefold:
- to contribute to China's social development and openness
- to serve as a channel between people and an ecumenical resource
- to make Christians' involvement and participation in the larger society better known to non-Christian Chinese people

Amity has received the support of friends in China and overseas. Its projects are a model of development in parts of China not deeply affected by the post-1978 economic reforms. Among Amity's commitments are the training of rural health-care workers, supporting rural medical clinics, building homes for the elderly, assisting with education for the hearing impaired, drilling wells for water, providing short-term training classes as in the treatment of the blind, and distributing relief packages containing quilts, clothes, and food to those living in areas struck by floods and other natural disasters.

Amity also addresses the needs of developing China through the Amity Teacher s Program. From an initial start in 1985 of 22 teachers in Nanjing, Amity now sponsors more than 80 foreign-language teachers in 50 institutions and middle schools in seven provinces and municipalities. "Every year we receive requests from schools and institutions in China to which we cannot send teachers—we just don't have enough," said Don Snow, Amity's educational program associate.

RARE MOMENTS

Greek mythology and the classical age of Greece were my emphases for the fall semester. My students had never heard of most of this material [and] we dug right in, studying history, philosophy, drama, heroes and heroines. It was not easy for the students to remember so much, and some resisted at first. I even got an anonymous note that said "All this is non-utilitarian." But I kept encouraging them. Finally they began to see parallels in their own lives. At the end of the semester, I introduced a 20th-century essay, "The Myth of Sisyphus," by Albert Camus. The bell rang. Like students all over the world, my Chinese students began to talk, to gather their books and to move out into the hall. But I looked down to see a quiet young man in the first row. He was staring at the floor, hands folded, eyes full of tears. He had been profoundly moved by the insights and inspirations of the essay. I went over to him and put my hands over his. He held my hands tightly, and though we spoke no words and hardly even looked at each other, I knew that he had been touched by the rare moment when life and literature are mutually affirming.[10]

The international community of language teachers has come from both ecumenical and denominational agencies in Australia, Austria, Belgium, Canada, Denmark, Finland, Germany, Japan, the Netherlands, New Zealand, Norway, Sweden, the Philippines, the United Kingdom, and the United States. The language courses taught are limited to English, German, and Japanese. Teachers work on two-year contracts, and some have extended their time to three, four, or more years. They report that the contact and rapport with their students bring much satisfaction, and they experience a feeling of having received more than they give.

Though candidates with training in language teaching and some knowledge of Chinese are generally better prepared for the experience, not all Amity teachers have had such backgrounds. What is more important is a willingness to learn, teach, adapt, and change. Patience, a cooperative spirit, and a good sense of humor are also essential assets!

The minimum requirements for teaching are an undergraduate degree and native or near-native competence in the language to be taught. Amity provides a small stipend and air fare, medical insurance, the summer briefings, and a small departure allowance for shipping. The school provides housing and sometimes food.

Encouraged to "live and serve in a way which brings credit" to their home churches, Amity teachers are also invited to identify themselves with Chinese Christians through participation in local churches. "This is not always an easy task," says Snow. "It often means sitting in a crowded room and listening to a sermon in a language you know only poorly, or not at all. But it does proclaim your faith and identify you with the Chinese church and the church universal that speaks louder than words."

"The sharing of Amity teachers is a wonderful opportunity for Christians to be involved in mission in ways largely determined by others rather than ourselves," comments the Rev. Ewing W. Carroll, Jr., executive secretary with the Asia Pacific Region, General Board of Global Ministries, The United Methodist Church. "In a day of incredible divisiveness, the Amity experience calls and challenges us to work together."

"Jesus Loves Me, This I Know, For the Bible Tells Me So"

The Bible is the second most widely published book in China, after the *Selected Works of Mao Zedong*. In urban and rural churches alike, a Bible for personal use and study is among a Christian's most valued possessions. Since 1987 the Nanjing Amity Printing Company, a joint venture with the United Bible Societies, has published 10 million of the 13 million copies of the Bible printed since 1980. The rest were printed on government presses before the Amity Printing Company was established. Standard, pocket-size, and large-character editions are printed as well as the New Testament in Chinese braille. There are also reference Bibles and Bibles in seven minority languages such as Korean, Mao, Lisu, and Jingpo.

The Amity Printing Company models ecumenism and the sharing of its resources by extending its operations to export Bibles, although exports are only a fraction of its total operation. In 1994 it printed 35,000 Bibles for export, including 15,000 children's Bibles for India, 10,000 Bibles in Jingpo and Lahu for Thailand, and 10,000 Bibles in Chinese, which the Hong Kong Bible Society distributed to Chinese living in Russia. In 1995 it printed several thousand Catholic reference Bibles for export to Spain.

Millions of copies of the *New Chinese Hymnal* have also been published along with devotional guides, biblical commentaries, inspirational meditations, and catechism information. The China Christian Council also uses the Amity Printing Company to print a three-booklet literacy primer, developed to teach illiterate church members how to read.

There is no need for well-intentioned but misinformed Christian travelers to smuggle Bibles into China. Such Bibles are destined to end up in customs warehouses alongside other smuggled goods. Such acts leave the false impression that Christianity is once again an instrument of foreign religious organizations and actually endanger the local Chinese Christians who must live and work within the laws of their country.

Packing Bibles at the Nanjing Amity Printing Company

Because of this problem, the China Christian Council has called for an end to the shipping and smuggling of Bibles into China, believing that the printing and distribution of Bibles within China is a much more effective way to meet the needs of Christian believers. "Why should Chinese Christians risk their freedom for a foreign Bible when they are legally available within China?" the Rev. Bao Jiyuan of the CCC told the HKCC in 1995.

Love in Action

The church in China today is alive and well. Chinese Christians have begun to see themselves in mission and are challenging Western Christians to rethink what mission is.

Prayer

Whenever Westerners visit with Chinese church leaders, the question they often pose is, "How can we help the Christian church in China?" Usually this question is asked in anticipation of receiving a kind of shopping list, since we in the West are often preoccupied with the "things" we have to share. Unexpectedly, the reply has been consistently simple and consistently profound: "Pray for us." The prayer request includes prayers for the church, its leadership, the Chinese people, and the church universal. As our understanding of mission deepens, so does our view of prayer.

Prayer is mission. It is the language that bonds Christians to God and the whole of creation. It becomes another means of sharing mutual love and communion with our worldwide neighbors. Prayer can go into places in God's world where we cannot.

As an example, the Hong Kong Christian Council is sponsoring a 1997 Global Prayer Chain for Hong Kong from 15 June to 15 July 1997. Christians around the world have been asked to pray for Hong Kong during this time of change in Hong Kong's sovereignty. To join in this prayer chain write the Hong Kong Christian Council, 33 Granville Road, 9/F, Kowloon, Hong Kong.

As Christians in China and Hong Kong have shown us, to be in mission is to be in relationship—with self, with others, with God.

Before Jesus gave us the Great Commission (Matt. 28:18-20) he taught us the Great Commandment, " 'You shall love the Lord your God

HOW LITERATE ARE YOU?

This is the first lesson in a simple textbook for illiterate rural Christians, written in simplified characters.[11]

Try reading this text. Get a feel of how it is to start your ABC's as an adult.

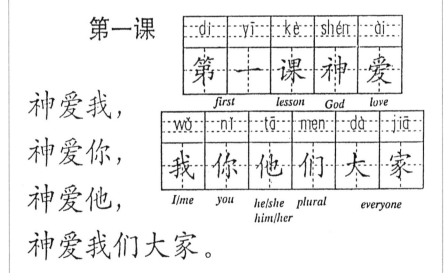

After reviewing the vocabulary words, you should be able to decipher the meaning of the text above.

with all your heart, and with all your soul, and with all your mind.' This is the greatest and first commandment. And a second is like it, 'You shall love your neighbor as yourself' [Matt. 22:37-39]."

The command to go and make disciples should always be based on loving God and loving one's neighbor. With love as a missional basis, reaching out and touching others produces some interesting and exciting possibilities.

Teaching English in China

Another way to express love in action is to teach English in a Chinese school or university. As explained previously, the Amity Teachers Program offers an enriching two-year teaching experience. It invites experienced and well-qualified teachers with and without degrees in teaching English to speakers of other languages (TESOL) to supplement local teachers.

Amity has increasingly focused on teacher-training institutions. By targeting Chinese teachers of English in rural areas, many of whom teach the subject without having heard a native accent or a fluent speaker, Amity hopes to affect an even greater number of people. For information, write your denominational mission agency or the China Program, National Council of the Churches of Christ, USA [NCCCUSA], Room 616, 475 Riverside Drive, New York, NY 10115. In Canada write Canada China Programme, 129 St. Clair Avenue West, Toronto, Ontario, M4V IN5.

Catholics in North America can teach English in China through Amity or through the Association for International Teaching, Educational and Curriculum Exchange. AITECE was founded in Hong Kong in 1988 under the sponsorship of the Columban Fathers Society as a medium for Christians in other countries to help in the modernization of China, especially education. It recruits language teachers to work in Chinese universities. For information write AITECE, 48 Princess Margaret Road, Homantin, Kowloon, Hong Kong. Recruiting for AITECE is also done through the United States Catholic China Bureau, Presidents Hall, Seton Hall University, South Orange, NJ 07079-2689. This Catholic body was founded in 1989 to foster friendship with the Chinese people and share their commitment to the values of the gospel.

Summer of Sharing

If you can't commit to two years in China, you might consider Summer of Sharing (SOS). SOS, sponsored by the China Program, NCCCUSA, is a summer program for young adults, ages 18 to 30. Its partner has been the Guangzhou YWCA. Through classroom sharing, using spoken English, and outdoor group activities, SOS facilitates friendships and bridge-building between young people in China and North America. Approximately 15 young adults from China are selected by the YWCA for this program of English-language immersion. Classroom exchange is augmented with outings to cultural and historical sites. Some volunteer work is scheduled, whether cleaning activity rooms at the Y or holding babies at a local orphanage. For North Americans, it is immersion in Chinese culture as they live, work, and share their lives at the Y.

Summer of Sharing also includes a week of travel and worship as a Christian Youth Camp, facilitated by provincial Christian councils. The experience attempts to give participants, both Chinese and North American, some understanding of the realities of the church in China and the importance it plays in the life of young Christians there. For information, write Summer of Sharing, Room 1533, 475 Riverside Drive, New York, NY 10115.

Study Tours and Travel

If seeing is believing, then experiencing surely leads toward increased understanding. Many denominations and their China programs offer study tours to China and Hong Kong as part of their mission to churches in North America. These tours usually last two to three weeks and provide a rich historical, cultural, and religious framework. Worship in local churches is usually enriched by conversations with local church leaders. No amount of talking or studying can replace worshiping with Christians in China and Hong Kong. Their steadfast and trusting spirit is a testimony that indeed God is ever faithful, ever sure.

Mission Education

By participating in this study focused on *The Enduring Church: Christians in China and Hong Kong*, you have participated in mission! Increase your knowledge by consulting sources listed in the Appendix. Think about ways you can share what you have learned with your local church. Study can help us understand the Chinese in their own society and the tasks and obstacles they face. Invite a former Amity teacher, Summer of Sharing participant, or China Program staff person to speak by coordinating a China/Hong Kong event. In the spirit of ecumenism, invite other church groups to share in this experience. Join in a World Day of Prayer, knowing that Christians in Hong Kong and China are in prayerful praise and worship with you on that same day.

Find out what audiovisual resources are available from your denominational offices or write to the China Program, NCCCUSA, Room 616, 475 Riverside Drive, New York, NY 10115. To keep further informed on

China-related news, especially as it applies to the church, subscribe to *China News Update, China Talk, Amity Newsletter,* and *Amity News Service* (see Appendix).

Assisting with Amity Projects

Sometimes being in mission also includes sharing our financial resources with others. A major ecumenical partner is the Amity Foundation, whose health, education, and social-service projects reach millions of Chinese. As a sign of Christian love and presence in China, Amity's Special Needs Fund enables you prayerfully and financially to assist programs such as the training of health-care workers, helping a child return to school, buying a family two goats that will supply livestock products and organic fertilizer, or providing a hearing aid and language training to a child who needs them. You can assist with the printing of Bibles and Christian literature for distribution in China through the Nanjing Amity Printing Company. Consult your denomination or the China Program, NCCCUSA.

Forward and Together into God's Future

Entering into the spirit and practice of mutuality in mission has implications that we can claim as blessings. First, we may be face to face with gospel forms that seem strange to us. If we are open, our encounter with people of another culture and their response in liturgy, theology, and polity will encourage our own deeper understanding with Jesus Christ. Second, we will have new experiences of dialogue, compromise, and consensus. Democracy, offering a voice to those who have had no voice, can be a powerful partner in the work of discernment. Third, more and more we will work ecumenically and interreligiously. We alone cannot carry out the tasks God calls us to do. There is joy in a shared journey. Fourth, we will learn the blessed lesson of not being in control. We will do the spiritual work of trying to overcome our fear of difference, our loathing of change, and our lust for control. Power shared reminds us that God is the Source. Lastly, we will realize that partnership is a very practical matter of common-sense stewardship.[12]

Jesus tells a story of neighbors, the one bleeding in the ditch and the one binding wounds with bandages and the oil of healing. This story offers clues for mission theology in the days ahead. If we can see ourselves as both blessed givers and blessed receivers, if we can be both bold and vulnerable, if we can offer respect and mutuality, mission partnership will lead us into God's future.[13]

1. Jonathan J. Bonk, *Mission and Money, Affluence as a Western Missionary Problem* (Maryknoll, N.Y.: Orbis Press, 1992), p. xii.
2. Ibid., p. 106
3. K. H. Ting, *No Longer Strangers, Selected Writings of K. H. Ting*, ed. Ray Whitehead (Maryknoll, NY: Orbis Press, 1989), p. 58.
4. Kenneth Guest, *Wind Across China* (Nashville: Graded Press, 1989), p. 68. For a fuller understanding of the empty-hands theology, see Frederick Wilson's *Ecumenical Sharing of Resources: Empty Hands*, Geneva: World Council of Churches.
5. Ting, *No Longer Strangers*, p. 96
6. "Gansu Christians Set Example," *Amity News Service*, August 1995, no. 95.4.3.
7. "Christian Village Sets Example," *Amity News Service*, February 1995, no. 95.1.5.
8. "Church-Run Store Sets Example," *Amity News Service*, December 1994, no. 94.6.7.
9. Ting, *No Longer Strangers,* p. 97.
10. Carol C. Walker, "Teaching for the Amity Foundation," *New World Outlook*, September-October 1994.
11. "How Literate Are You?" *China Talk*, April 1993.
12. K. Almond, "Neighbors in Mission," *Partnership, A Newsletter for Church in Mission*, fall 1993.
13. Ibid.

HISTORY OF IMPERIAL CHINA

Time of Huangdi
(Yellow Emperor)
c. 2700 B.C.

• Agricultural villages; beginning of Chinese civilization in the Yellow River region

Xia
2100-1600 B.C.

• Emphasis on community; respect for elderly

Shang
1600-1100 B.C.

• Written language on oracle bones; calendar based on moon

Zhou
1100-221 B.C.

• City states • Period of sages (Confucius, Mencius, Lao Tzu and Daoism, Chuang Tzu, Mo Tzu, Hanfei Tzu)

Qin
221-206 B.C.

• Unification of China; Great Wall; terra cotta soldiers

Han
206 B.C.-220 A.D.

• Confucianism the state philosophy; start of history writing
• Introduction of Buddhism (67 A.D.)

North-South
420-489

• Literature, music, mathematics • Examination system for civil service

Sui
581-681

• Grand Canal from Beijing to Hangzhou (1,200 miles)

Tang
618-907

• Age of peace, prosperity, poetry, and religious tolerance • Silk Road from Chang-an to Antioch, Syria • Introduction of Nestorian Christianity (635); Buddhist scripture brought from India (645); Jian Zhen, Buddhist monk, missionary to Japan (751)

Song
960-1279

• Invention of printing, compass, and magnet • Arrival of Marco Polo from Venice (1260) • Neo-Confucianism (Chu Hsi) influenced by Buddhism and Daoism

Yuan
1279-1368

• China conquered by Mongols • Arrival of John of Montecorvino (1294), later bishop of Beijing, and other Franciscan missionaries

Ming
1368-1644

• Expeditions to Southeast and South Asia; exchange of goods and ideas with 39 countries • Arrival of Portuguese in Macau (1514), which became a Portuguese colony (1555); arrival of Matteo Ricci and Jesuits in Macau (1593) and Beijing (1601)

Qing 1644-1911	• China conquered by Manchus • First Opium War (1839-42); Treaty of Nanking (1842) ceding Hong Kong to Britain, the first of some 1,000 Unequal Treaties carving up China among Western powers and Japan • Taiping Rebellion (1851-64) of peasants, influenced by Christianity, against the corrupt Qing court; considered heretical by the West, resulted in 20 million deaths • After Anglo-French invasion (1860) Kowloon Peninsula ceded to Britain by Convention of Peking • After First Sino-JapaneseWar (1894) Taiwan ceded to Japan • Qingdao ceded to Germany (1897) • Failure of "Hundred Days Reform" by intellectuals (1898); power seized by Empress Dowager; New Territories and 235 islands around Hong Kong leased to Britain by Second Convention of Peking • Boxer Rebellion (1900) against Western ideas and Chinese Christians; occupation of Beijing by 18,000 troops from eight Western nations • End of the examination system for civil service (1905)

HISTORY OF MODERN CHINA

Republic 1911-49	• Revolution (October 1911) led by Sun Yat-Sen, end of imperial rule • May Fourth Movement (1919), student demonstration protesting Western treatment of China after World War I; anti-Confucianism (blaming "feudalistic" traditions for China's lack of progress); language reform; women's movement • Founding of Chinese Communist Party (CCP) in Shanghai (July 1921) • Church of Christ in China (1927) formed by most mainline Protestant denominations • After break between Nationalists (KMT) and Communists (CCP), Mao Zedong forced into Jiangxi mountains, where he experimented in land reform; CCP Long March (1934) from Jiangxi on foot; after years, thousands of miles, and tens of thousands of deaths, arrival in Yanan, Shaanxi Province, new base of the Communist revolution • Japanese occupation of Manchuria and establishment of Manchukuo; Second Sino-Japanese War (1937-45), Hong Kong bombed by Japan (Dec. 1941); under Japanese occupation till defeat of Japan in World War II (1945); abolition of Unequal Treaties (1942) • Civil war between KMT and CCP (1944); flight of some 1 million refugees to Hong Kong; defeat of KMT, which retreated to Taiwan (1949)
People's Republic 1949-	• Mao Zedong's declaration, "The Chinese people have stood up" (1949) • Beginning of land reform, new system of food distribution, health service, and new marriage law • Great Leap Forward (1958-60) to force rapid industrialization; failure • Explosion of China's first nuclear device (1964) • Great Proletarian Cultural Revolution (1966-76) controlled by extreme leftists; persecution of intellectuals; closing of schools, churches,

mosques, temples • "Ping-Pong" diplomacy as U.S.-China relations thawed (1971), visit of U.S. President Richard Nixon (1972) • Death of Mao Zedong and other leaders; Tangshan earthquake with 650,000 casualties; "Gang of Four" arrested • Deng Xiaoping in power (1977); effort of "Four Modernizations" • Beginning of reforms (1978) leading to demise of communes; normalization of U.S.-China relations announced by Jimmy Carter • Beginning of negotiations on future of Hong Kong (1982); Chinese guarantee of Hong Kong's system unchanged for 50 years after reversion (1983); Sino-British Joint Declaration that Hong Kong will revert to China on 1 July 1997 (1984); first indirect elections to the Legislative Council in Hong Kong (1985) • Student demonstration in Tiananmen Square (1989); military crackdown • The Basic Law, a mini-constitution for the future Hong Kong, promulgated by China's congress (1990); Sino-British agreement on the new Hong Kong airport construction (1991); end of British rule of Hong Kong (30 June 1997)

Prepared by Jean Woo for Map 'n' Facts: China and Hong Kong, © 1996 by Friendship Press.

REGULATION GOVERNING THE RELIGIOUS ACTIVITIES OF FOREIGN NATIONALS WITHIN CHINA

Decree No. 144 of the State Council of the People's Republic of China signed by Premier Li Peng, 31 January 1994

Article 1. In order to protect the freedom of religious belief of foreign nationals in China and to safeguard the public interest, this regulation is formulated in conformity with the Constitution.

Article 2. The People's Republic of China respects the religious freedom of foreign nationals in China and protects friendly visits, cultural and scholarly exchanges, and other such religious activities between foreign nationals and religious circles in China.

Article 3. Foreign nationals may participate in religious activities in religious venues in China, including monasteries, temples, mosques, and churches; and, at the invitation of a religious body at or above the provincial, autonomous region, or municipality level, may discuss the scriptures and preach.

Article 4. Foreign nationals may hold religious activities for other foreign nationals at venues recognized by the Religious Affairs Bureaus of the People's Government at or above the county level.

Article 5. Foreign nationals in China may request Chinese clergy to perform religious rites such as baptisms, marriages, funerals, and Taoist and Buddhist rituals.

Article 6. When foreign nationals enter China, they may carry printed materials, audio and visual materials, and other religious items for their own use; if these are brought in quantities which exceed those for personal use, such items will be dealt with according to the relevant Chinese customs regulations. Religious publications and religious audio and visual materials whose content is harmful to the public interest are forbidden.

Article 7. Foreign nationals recruiting students within China for overseas religious studies or who come to China to study or teach in Chinese religious educational institutions are subject to the relevant Chinese regulations.

Article 8. Foreign nationals who engage in religious activities in China must respect Chinese laws and regulations. They are not permitted to establish religious organization liaison office venues for religious activities or run religious schools and institutes within China. They are not allowed to recruit believers among the Chinese citizenry, appoint clergy, or undertake evangelistic activities.

Article 9. The Bureaus of Religious Affairs at or above the county level or other offices concerned should act to dissuade and put a stop to religious activities of foreign nationals which violate this regulation. If the violation constitutes an immigration offense or a matter of public security, the public security organs will dispense penalties according to the law. If the violation constitutes a crime, the judiciary will investigate to determine where criminal responsibility lies.

Article 10. This regulation will be applied to the religious activities of foreign organizations within China.

Article 11. The religious activities in mainland China of Chinese citizens residing overseas, or residents of Taiwan, Hong Kong, and Macau will be subject to this regulation.

Article 12. Interpretation of this regulation will lie with the Religious Affairs Bureau of the State Council.

Article 13. This regulation takes effect from the date of issue.

REGULATION GOVERNING VENUES FOR RELIGIOUS ACTIVITIES

Decree No. 145 of the State Council of the People's Republic of China signed by Premier Li Peng, 31 January 1994

Article 1. In order to protect normal religious activities, safeguard the legal rights of venues for religious activities, and facilitate the management of these venues, the following regulation has been formulated in conformity with the Constitution.

Article 2. For the purposes of this regulation, "venues for religious activities" refers to monasteries, temples, mosques, churches, and other fixed venues. Registration is required for the establishment of a venue for religious activities. The registration procedure will be decided by the Religious Affairs Bureau of the State Council.

Article 3. The management of venues for religious activities will be undertaken by the venue's own management team. Its legal rights and the normal religious activities which take place there will be under the protection of law and no organization or person will be permitted to transgress or interfere.

Article 4. Venues for religious activities should set up a management system. Religious activities undertaken in these venues should comply with the laws and regulations. No person shall be permitted to make use of any such venue to undertake activities which harm national unity, ethnic unity, or the social order, harm citizens' health, or obstruct the national educational system. Venues for religious activities shall not be controlled by persons or organizations outside China.

Article 5. Persons normally resident in venues for religious activities or those temporarily resident must comply with State regulations on household registration.

Article 6. Venues for religious activities may accept from their adherents voluntary offerings of alms, donations, and contributions. In accepting donations from persons and organizations outside China, venues for religious activities shall act in accordance with relevant regulations.

Article 7. Within their premises, venues for religious activities may, complying with State regulations, offer for sale religious articles, artwork, and publications.

Article 8. The property and income of a religious venue shall be subject to management and use by the venue's management team and shall not be held or gratuitously transferred to any other unit or person.

Article 9. The closing or merger of religious venues should be recorded with the registration organization and its property dealt with according to the relevant State regulations.

Article 10. The land, mountains, forests, or buildings administered by a religious venue should be documented in compliance with relevant State regulations by the management team of the venue or the religious body to which it is subject.

The State may requisition land, mountain and forest land, buildings, and so on, managed and used by a religious venue in compliance with the "PRC Property Administration Law" and other relevant State regulations.

Article 11. Relevant units or persons who, within the premises of a venue administered by a religious venue, build or renovate buildings, set up commercial or social-service enterprises, or hold a display or exhibition, or make films or television programs, etc., are required to secure the permission of the management team of the religious venue in question and that of the Religious Affairs Bureau of the People's Government at or above county level before applying to the departments concerned.

Article 12. Religious venues which have been listed as protected cultural relics or which are located in scenic areas must comply with the stipulations of relevant laws and regulations on administering and protecting cultural relics and the environment and must accept the guidance and supervision of departments concerned.

Article 13. The Religious Affairs Bureau of the People's Government at or above the county level shall undertake guidance and supervision in the administration of these regulations.

Article 14. If a religious venue violates the stipulations of this regulation, the Religious Affairs Bureau of the People's Government at, or above, county level may apply penalties according to the seriousness of the case, issue a warning, halt activities, or rescind registration. If the case is especially serious, it may be submitted to the corresponding level of the People's Government, which may ban the venue.

Article 15. If violation of the stipulations of this regulation constitute an act in violation of public security, the public security organs shall mete out penalties in accordance with the relevant regulations of the PRC Public Security Administration Penal Code; if the violation constitutes a criminal act, the judiciary shall undertake an investigation to determine criminal responsibility.

Article 16. If the parties concerned decide not to comply with the administrative methods (of dealing with the case), they may, in compliance with relevant laws and regulations, apply for administrative reconsideration or institute administrative litigation.

Article 17. If a violation of these regulations involves infringement of the legal rights of a religious venue, then the Religious Affairs Bureau of the People's Government at the county level or above will ask the People's Government at the corresponding level to put a halt to this infringement of rights; if the violation constitutes an economic loss, the losses should be made good in compliance with the law.

Article 18. The People's Government at the provincial, autonomous region, and municipality level may, in compliance with this regulation, formulate practical measures on the basis of local realities.

Article 19. Interpretation of this regulation lies with the Religious Affairs Bureau of the State Council.

Article 20. This regulation takes effect on the date of issue.

REGISTRATION PROCEDURES FOR VENUES FOR RELIGIOUS ACTIVITIES

Article 1. These Procedures are formulated in accordance with Article 2 of the "Regulation Governing Venues for Religious Activities."

Article 2. The following conditions must be met to establish a venue for religious activity:

1) There must be a fixed place and name;
2) There must be citizens who are religious believers who regularly take part in religious activities;
3) There must be a management organization composed of citizens who are religious believers;
4) There must be professional clergy or persons who meet the requirements of the particular religious group to conduct religious services;
5) There must be management regulations;
6) There must be a legal source of income.

Article 3. At the time of application for registration, the venue for religious activity must provide the following documentation:

1) An application form;
2) Documentation and credentials related to the venue;
3) The opinion of the village (or township) People's Government or of the city neighborhood committee.

Article 4. The head of the venue's management organization must submit the application for registration, together with the materials required under Article 3, to the Religious Affairs Department of the People's Government at the county level or above.

Article 5. Upon receipt of an application for registration and related materials, the Religious Affairs Department of the People's Government at the county level or above must make a decision on whether to consider the application within 15 days, on the basis of whether the materials are complete.

Article 6. The Religious Affairs Department of the People's Government at the county level or above will, within 60 days of the decision to consider the application, grant registration and issue a registration certificate to those venues which, based upon investigation and the opinions of related parties, comply with the regulations found in Articles 2 and 3 of these Procedures, and with related provisions in the "Regulation Governing Venues for Religious Activities." Venues which do not fully comply with the regulations will, upon review, be granted temporary registration or deferred registration or be denied registration. They will be notified in writing and given an explanation for the decision.

Article 7. Religious venues registered before the promulgation of these procedures must exchange their certificate; those which have not been registered should apply for registration according to these Procedures.

Article 8. If a religious venue closes, merges, moves, or otherwise changes the terms which applied at the time of application, its management organization must apply for modification of the certificate to the original issuing body.

Article 9. According to the regulations of the "General Civil Law," legally registered venues for religious activities which qualify as juridical persons and which at the same time apply to register as juridical persons, will be issued a certificate of registration as juridical persons. According to the law, a religious venue as a juridical person independently enjoys civil rights and takes on civil responsibilities.

114

Article 10. A venue's certificate of registration and certificate of registration as a juridical person, cannot be changed, transferred, or lent. If the certificate is lost, the venue should report its loss promptly to the original issuing body and apply for a replacement.

Article 11. Upon being granted registration, a venue for religious activity must submit an annual management report to the Religious Affairs Department of the government during the first quarter of each year.

Article 12. The certificate of registration for venues of religious activities and related forms will be uniform and will be issued by the Religious Affairs Bureau of the State Council.

Article 13. Matters not regulated by these Procedures follow the "Regulation Governing Venues for Religious Activities."

Article 14. Interpretation of these Procedures is the provenance of the Religious Affairs Bureau of the State Council.

Article 15. These Procedures take effect from the date of promulgation.

BASIC LAW OF THE HONG KONG SPECIAL ADMINISTRATIVE REGION OF THE PEOPLE'S REPUBLIC OF CHINA

Article 140. The Government of the HKSAR shall not restrict the freedom of religious belief, interfere in the internal affairs of religious organizations, or restrict religious activities which do not contravene the laws of the Region.

Religious organizations shall, in accordance with law, enjoy the rights to acquire, use, dispose of, and inherit property and the right to receive financial assistance. Their previous property rights and interests shall be maintained and protected.

Religious organizations may, according to their previous practice, continue to run seminaries and other schools, hospitals, and welfare institutions and to provide other social services.

Religious organizations and believers in the HKSAR may maintain and develop their relations with religious organizations and believers elsewhere.

Article 147. The relationship between non-governmental organizations in fields such as education, science, technology, culture, art, sports, the professions, medicine and health, labour, social welfare, and social work as well as religious organizations in the HKSAR and their counterparts on the mainland shall be based on the principles of non-subordination, non-interference, and mutual respect.

Article 148. Non-governmental organizations in fields such as education, science, technology, culture, art, sports, the professions, medicine and health, labour, social welfare, and social work as well as religious organizations in the HKSAR may maintain and develop relations with foreign countries and other regions and with relevant international organizations. They may, as required, use the name "Hong Kong, China" in relevant activities.

THE MAIN POINTS OF THE SINO-BRITISH JOINT DECLARATION ON THE QUESTION OF HONG KONG, signed by Britain and China 1984

A. The *recovery* of Hong Kong by China "is the common aspiration of the entire Chinese people." Sovereignty will be *resumed* on July 1, 1997

B. The United Kingdom declares it will restore Hong Kong to China on July 1, 1997.

C. China declares the following 12 points:

1. Hong Kong will be governed as a Special Administrative Region;
2. The HKSAR will be directly under the Central Chinese Government and, except in matters of foreign affairs and defense, will have a high degree of autonomy;
3. The HKSAR will have its own executive and legislative structures and an independent judiciary;
4. The HKSAR is to be run by local Hong Kong Chinese. The chief executive, on the basis of elections or consultations held in Hong Kong, will be appointed by Beijing;
5. Hong Kong's socio-economic system with rights of ownership such as private property, enterprise, and inheritance, will remain the same;
6. Hong Kong will remain a free port with a separate custom service;
7. Hong Kong will retain its status as an international financial center with free flow of capital;
8. Hong Kong's tax structure will remain independent with no taxes levied from Beijing;
9. Hong Kong will continue to carry on and develop further economic ties with Britain and other countries;
10. As Hong Kong, China, the SAR may develop economic and cultural ties with other regions;
11. Public order will be the responsibility of the SAR government;
12. Policies stipulated in the Joint Declaration will be in force for 50 years until 2047.

GLOSSARY OF ORGANIZATIONS AND TERMS

Amity Foundation, founded in 1985, was created on the initiative of Christians in China as an independent Chinese voluntary organization to engage in health, education, rural development, and social welfare in China.

Association for International Teaching, Educational, and Curriculum Exchange (AITEC) is a Catholic organization founded in 1988 in Hong Kong as a way for Christians to help modernize China, especially in education.

Basic Law of the Hong Kong Special Administrative Region of the People's Republic of China, issued in 1990, states the conditions for the government of Hong Kong as of 1 July 1997.

Caritas is the umbrella organization for Catholic charities in Hong Kong.

China Christian Council (CCC), founded in 1980, is a voluntary association of Chinese Christians that works at national, provincial, and local levels to coordinate Protestant church affairs, train leaders, print Bibles, and deal with pastoral matters.

Chinese Catholic Bishops' Conference (CBC), restructured in 1980, is an organization of Catholic bishops to administer the Catholic Church in China.

Chinese Catholic Church Administration Commission (CAC), founded in 1980 by the Catholic Church in China, is a voluntary administrative organization to serve Catholics in China.

Chinese Protestant Three-Self Patriotic Movement: *See* Three-Self Patriotic Movement.

Christian Action (formerly Hong Kong Aid to Refugees) is a voluntary association that cooperates with the government of Hong Kong on social-service projects such as retraining workers and aiding Vietnam refugees.

Decree No. 144 Regulation Governing the Religious Activities of Foreign Nationals With China, was issued by the State Council of the PRC in 1991.

Decree No. 145 Regulations Governing Venues for Religious Activities, was issued by the State Council of the PRC in 1991.

Hong Kong Chinese Christian Churches Union, founded in 1915, is a voluntary association with 259 member congregations.

Hong Kong Christian Council (HKCC), founded in 1954, is a voluntary association that has 19 member denominations. It has many committees, including a women's committee, and works with many church-related groups.

Hong Kong Christian Industrial Committee (CIC) is a committee of the HKCC that aids industrial workers in labor concerns and justice issues.

Hong Kong Christian Service is the social-service arm of the HKCC.

Hong Kong Women's Christian Council (HKWCC) is an independent voluntary association that addresses issues of gender equality in the church and society.

Meeting point, in China, one of some 30,000 worshiping congregations that gather in homes, courtyards, halls, or other locations. Led by lay persons, most meeting points are linked to a church, which usually sends a pastor to administer the sacraments.

Religious Affairs Bureau (RAB) is an office of the State Council of the PRC that acts as a liaison between the five basic religions and the government, especially in situations where the policy of religious freedom has been violated or property is to be returned to religious bodies.

Three-Self Patriotic Movement (TSPM) Committee, founded in 1954 as all denominational structures went out of existence, is a Protestant organization that is a bridge between the Christian community and the Religious Affairs Bureau. It promotes the three principles of self-government, self-support, and self-propagation that guide the Chinese Protestant churches.

Venue, according to Decrees no. 144 and 145, is (1) a fixed place with a name, (2) where citizens . . . regularly take part in religious activities, (3) with a management . . . composed of citizens who are religious believers, (4) with management regulations, (5) with professional clergy or persons who meet the requirements of the particular religious group to conduct services. It includes both churches and meeting points.

CHINESE CHARACTERS, CHINESE NAMES, AND ROMANIZATION

For centuries, written Chinese consisted of thousands of complex characters that were difficult to learn. Only a small portion of the population had the education that was necessary. In the 20th century, as part of the PRC government's effort to educate everyone, some of the most commonly used characters were simplified. In Taiwan and Hong Kong, however, the complex characters are still used.

Traditionally Chinese characters are read in vertical rows from top to bottom and from right to left across a page. In the late 20th century many publications are printed to be read horizontally from left to right, as in European languages. In China, Hong Kong, and Taiwan, both the vertical and horizontal systems are used, the horizontal system more so in China.

In referring to people, the Chinese give the surname first followed by the personal name. Thus in Mao Zedong, Mao is the surname. Some Chinese have adopted the English style of giving the personal name or initials first, for example, K. H. Ting. This book uses the Chinese form except in a few instances where the person is better known in the English form, such as K. H. Ting for Ding Guangzun, or some other Western form, such as Confucius for the ancient philosopher Kong Zi (Kong Sage, or Wise Man).

Western scholars had to devise a way to convert the sounds of Chinese characters into roman letters that Westerners could read. Several systems of transliteration evolved. For years the Wade–Giles system was commonly used, resulting in such familiar spellings as Taoism, Chiang Kai-Shek, Mao Tse-Tung, and Chou En-Lai. The PRC government adopted the *pinyin* system as closer to the Chinese pronunciation. In most cases the *pinyin* version is easy to read and speak: Daoism, Mao Zedong, and Chou Enlai. Hong Kong and Taiwan still use the Wade–Giles system. This book uses *pinyin* for names in China and Wade–Giles for those in Hong Kong and Taiwan.

GLOSSARY OF CHINESE CHURCH LEADERS IN THIS BOOK

Bao Jiayuan° Associate general secretary of the China Christian Council (CCC) and director of its Nanjing Office in charge of international relations

Cai Wenhao° (Peter Tsai, 1913-1993) Former vice president of CCC; president of Zhejiang Christian Council; chair of Zhejiang TSPM; principal of Zhejiang Seminary; pastor, educator, and hymn writer

Cao Shengjie°† A vice president of the CCC; pastor of Huai'en (Grace) Church of Shanghai, vice chair of the Commission on Women's Work, CCC

Cheng Jingyi Leader of the national church and ecumenical movement in the early 20th century

Deng Yuzhi† (Cora Deng) Outstanding leader of women's movement in China, former general secretary of the national YWCA, and one of the founders of the TSPM Committee in 1954

Gan Xianzhen† YWCA leader in Shanghai; elder, Huxi Church of Shanghai

Gao Ying°† 1985 graduate of Nanjing Theological Seminary; M.A. (1991),Graduate Theological Union, Berkeley; executive secretary, Commission on Women's Work, CCC; pastor of Chongwenmen Church, Beijing

Han Wenzao Acting general secretary of CCC; general secretary of the Amity Foundation; member of the national Chinese People's Political Consultative Conference

Jiang Peifen† (1915-1995) Evangelical leader well known as "Elder Sister Jiang"; teacher of Old Testament, Nanjing Theological Seminary; author of many books for the training of rural church workers

Lin De'en° General secretary, Jiangsu Provincial Christian Council

Pen Cui'an† 1986 graduate of Nanjing Theological Seminary; M.A. (1991), University of Birmingham, England; first woman vice principal of Nanjing Theological Seminary

Shen Yifan° (1928-1994) Consecrated bishop in Shanghai (1988); executive vice president, CCC; head, Commission on Theological Education, CCC

Shi Qigui° Senior pastor, Mu'en Church of Shanghai; hymn writer ("I Love the Church in China" being best known)

Su Deci° Associate general secretary, CCC; dean, Huadong Theological Seminary, Shanghai; chair, Commission on Theological Education, CCC; M.A. (1992), Wesley Theological Seminary, Washington, D.C.

Sun Yanli° (1915-1995) Former principal, Huadong Theological Seminary; senior pastor of Mu'en Church; consecrated bishop in Shanghai, 1988

Ting, K. H.° (Ding Guangxun, bishop) President, CCC; chair, TSPM; president, Nanjing Theological Seminary; president, Board of Directors, the Amity Foundation; vice chair, national CPPCC; secretary, World Students Christian Federation (WSCF) in Geneva (1948-50)

Wang Weifan° Poet, philosopher, theologian, hymn writer ("Winter Is Past"); author of devotional book *Lilies of the Field*; teacher at Nanjing Theological Seminary

Wu, Yaozong (Y. T. Wu, 1893-1979) Former general secretary of National YMCA; a founder of TSPM Committee in 1954 and secretary general of TSPM till 1979

Zhao Zichen° (T. C. Chao, 1888-1979) Former president of Yanjing School of Theology, Beijing; one of the presidents of the World Council of Churches (elected in 1948); theologian, philosopher, and writer of many hymns in the 1930s (including "Rise to Greet the Sun")

Zheng Yugui° President, Fujian Provincial Christian Council; principal, Fujian Theological Seminary in Fuzhou

    °   Ordained clergy   †   Woman

RESOURCES

Books

Carino, Theresa C., and Aileen S. P. Baviera, eds. *Black Cat, White Cat: An Inside View of Reform and Revolution in China* (Philippine-China Development Resource Center, 23 Madison Street, New Manila, Quezon City, Philippines).

Endicott, Stephen. *The Red Dragon: China, 1949-1990* (Kingston, Ontario: Ronald P. Frye & Co., 1991).

Fairbank, John K. *China: A New History* (Cambridge: Harvard University Press, 1992).

———. *The Great Chinese Revolution, 1800-1985* (New York: Harper & Row, 1986).

Fairbank, John K., and Edwin O. Reischauer. *China: Tradition and Transformation* (Boston: George Allen & Unwin, 1979).

Gernet, Jacques. *China and the Christian Impact* (New York: Cambridge University Press, 1985). Analysis of the missionary movement.

Hayhoe, Ruth, ed. *Education and Modernization: The Chinese Experience* (Tarrytown, N.Y.: Pergamon Press, 1992).

Hersey, John. *The Call: An American Missionary in China* (New York: Doubleday, 1989). Fiction in a historically accurate setting.

Holm, Bill. *Coming Home Crazy: An Alphabet of Chinese Essays* (Minneapolis: Milkweed Editions, 1990). Experiences of an American teacher in China in the 1980s.

Hu Wenzhong and Cornelius L. Grove. *Encountering the Chinese: A Guide for Americans* (Yarmouth, Me.: Intercultural Press, 1991). Used by Amity teachers and participants in SOS.

Kuo Siumay. *Journeying Through the Bible* (Nanjing: Nanjing University Press, 1990).

Lernoux, Penny. *Hearts on Fire* (Maryknoll, N.Y.: Orbis Books, 1993). History of Catholicism in China, especially the Maryknoll orders.

MacInnis, Donald E. *Religion in China Today: Policy and Practice* (Maryknoll, N.Y.: Orbis Books, 1989). Translations of Chinese documents in historical context.

Morris, Jan. *Hong Kong: Epilogue to an Empire* (New York: Penguin Books, 1989).

Ross, Andrew C. *A Vision Betrayed: The Jesuits in Japan and China, 1542-1742* (Maryknoll, N.Y.: Orbis Books, 1994).

Spence, Jonathan. *The Search for Modern China* (New York: W. W. Norton & Co., 1990).

Stepanchuk, Carol, and Charles Wong. *Mooncakes and Hungry Ghosts: Festivals of China* (China Books and Periodicals, 2929 24th Street, San Francisco, CA 94110, 1991).

Stockwell, Foster. *Religions in China Today* (Beijing: New World Press, 1993). (Available from China Books and Periodicals, 2929 24th Street, San Francisco, CA 94110.)

Tang, Edmond, and Jean-Paul Weist, eds. *The Catholic Church in Modern China* (Maryknoll, N.Y.: Orbis Books, 1993).

Terrill, Ross. *China in Our Time* (New York: Simon & Schuster, 1992).

Ting, K. H. *How to Study the Bible* (Hong Kong: Tao Fong Shan Economical Centre, 1981).

———— . *No Longer Strangers: Selected Writings of K. H. Ting*, ed. Raymond L. Whitehead (Maryknoll, N.Y.: Orbis Books, 1989).

Tuchman, Barbara. *Stillwell and the American Experience in China* (New York: Macmillan, 1971).

Wang Weifan. *Lilies of the Field* (Nashville: Upper Room, 1993). A book of devotional material.

Whyte, Bob. *Unfinished Encounter: China and Christianity* (London: Collins, 1988). Historical analysis.

Wickeri, Philip L. *Seeking the Common Ground: Protestant Christianity, the Three-Self Movement, and China's United Front* (Maryknoll, N.Y.: Orbis Books, 1989). Coexistence of patriotism and faith.

Zhang Xinxin and San Ye. *Chinese Profiles* (Beijing: Panda, 1986). Chinese people talking about themselves.

Periodicals

The Amity Newsletter, Amity Foundation Overseas Coordination Office, 4 Jordan Road, Kowloon, Hong Kong.

The Amity News Service, Amity Foundation Overseas Coordination Office, 4 Jordan Road, Kowloon, Hong Kong.

China News Update, Presbyterian Church (USA), 100 Witherspoon Street, Louisville, KY 40202.

China and Ourselves, Canada China Programme, 129 St. Clair Avenue West, Toronto, Ontario M4V IN5.

China Study Journal, Department for China Relations and Study, Council of Churches for Britain and Ireland, Inter-Church House, 35-41 Lower Marsh, London SE1 7RL. Covers all religions in China.

China Talk, Newsletter of the United Methodist China Program, Hong Kong China Liaison Office, United Methodist Church, 2 Man Wan Road, C-17, Kowloon, Hong Kong.

China Today, China International Book Trading Corp., P.O. Box 399, Beijing. A Chinese publication in English.

Chinese Theological Review, Foundation for Theological Education in Southeast Asia, 2390 Orchard, Holland, MI 49423. Translations from Chinese Protestant scholars.

Tapestries of Bible stories may be ordered from Amity Foundation, 17 Da Jian Yin Xiang, Nanjing; Tao Fong Shan Christian Centre, P.O. Box 33, Shatin, N.T. Hong Kong; Welfare Handicrafts Shops, Salisbury Road, Tsim Sha Tsui, Kowloon, Hong Kong.